Barthes: A Very Short Introduction

VERY SHORT INTRODUCTIONS are for anyone wanting a stimulating and accessible way in to a new subject. They are written by experts, and have been published in more than 25 languages worldwide.

The series began in 1995, and now represents a wide variety of topics in history, philosophy, religion, science, and the humanities. Over the next few years it will grow to a library of around 200 volumes – a Very Short Introduction to everything from ancient Egypt and Indian philosophy to conceptual art and cosmology.

Very Short Introductions available now:

Available soon:

AFRICAN HISTORY
  John Parker and Richard Rathbone
ANCIENT EGYPT   Ian Shaw
THE BRAIN   Michael O'Shea
BUDDHIST ETHICS
  Damien Keown
CHAOS   Leonard Smith
CHRISTIANITY   Linda Woodhead
CITIZENSHIP   Richard Bellamy
CLASSICAL ARCHITECTURE
  Robert Tavernor
CLONING   Arlene Judith Klotzko
CONTEMPORARY ART
  Julian Stallabrass
THE CRUSADES
  Christopher Tyerman
DERRIDA   Simon Glendinning
DESIGN   John Heskett
DINOSAURS   David Norman
DREAMING   J. Allan Hobson
ECONOMICS   Partha Dasgupta
THE END OF THE WORLD
  Bill McGuire
EXISTENTIALISM   Thomas Flynn
THE FIRST WORLD WAR
  Michael Howard
FREE WILL   Thomas Pink
FUNDAMENTALISM
  Malise Ruthven
HABERMAS   Gordon Finlayson

HIEROGLYPHS
  Penelope Wilson
HIROSHIMA   B. R. Tomlinson
HUMAN EVOLUTION
  Bernard Wood
INTERNATIONAL RELATIONS
  Paul Wilkinson
JAZZ   Brian Morton
MANDELA   Tom Lodge
MEDICAL ETHICS
  Tony Hope
THE MIND   Martin Davies
MYTH   Robert Segal
NATIONALISM   Steven Grosby
PERCEPTION   Richard Gregory
PHILOSOPHY OF RELIGION
  Jack Copeland and Diane Proudfoot
PHOTOGRAPHY
  Steve Edwards
THE RAJ   Denis Judd
THE RENAISSANCE
  Jerry Brotton
RENAISSANCE ART
  Geraldine Johnson
SARTRE   Christina Howells
THE SPANISH CIVIL WAR
  Helen Graham
TRAGEDY   Adrian Poole
THE TWENTIETH CENTURY
  Martin Conway

For more information visit our web site
www.oup.co.uk/vsi

Jonathan Culler

BARTHES

A Very Short Introduction

OXFORD
UNIVERSITY PRESS

OXFORD
UNIVERSITY PRESS

Great Clarendon Street, Oxford OX2 6DP

Oxford University Press is a department of the University of Oxford.
It furthers the University's objective of excellence in research, scholarship,
and education by publishing worldwide in

Oxford New York

Auckland Bangkok Buenos Aires Cape Town Chennai
Dar es Salaam Delhi Hong Kong Istanbul Karachi Kolkata
Kuala Lumpur Madrid Melbourne Mexico City Mumbai Nairobi
São Paulo Shanghai Taipei Tokyo Toronto

Oxford is a registered trade mark of Oxford University Press
in the UK and in certain other countries

Published in the United States
by Oxford University Press Inc., New York

First published by Fontana in 1983
First published as a Very Short Introduction 2002

British Library Cataloguing in Publication Data
Data available

Library of Congress Cataloging in Publication Data
Data available
ISBN 978-0-19-280159-3

7 9 10 8

Typeset by RefineCatch Ltd, Bungay, Suffolk
Printed in Great Britain by
Ashford Colour Press Ltd, Gosport, Hampshire

Contents

Preface to this edition

When Roland Barthes died in 1980, he was a formidable figure on the cultural and critical scene: a powerful presence, a commentator on everything under the sun, and a distinguished eminence of an avant-garde that had radically transformed the humanities in general and literary studies in particular. Twenty years later, his status has become more enigmatic. What is Roland Barthes for us today? What sort of author or intellectual force? Perhaps the question should be, rather, what Barthes should we read and why? Barthes's longtime publisher, Seuil, has issued his complete works in a hefty three-volume edition of several thousand pages, which makes his hundreds of short, occasional pieces as available as his most famous books. His last book, *La Chambre claire*, a provocative, idiosyncratic, personal essay on photography, is much cited, praised, and debated. His early *Mythologies* is a formative work in cultural studies and a reference point in debates about the nature of this field. Many of the books and essays in between – particularly *S/Z* and *Le Plaisir du texte* – are read in college and university courses on literary criticism or literary theory. Is Barthes a literary theorist? As a homosexual who never openly declared himself and who left only a couple of brief posthumous texts about his sexual life, Barthes has also provoked interest in the field of gay and lesbian studies. And his autobiographical *Roland Barthes par Roland Barthes* remains an extraordinarily seductive and stimulating book, one of the most engaging we have about the adventures of thought and writing. If only because of the question of what to read, the need for an assessment of Barthes and his contribution is greater than ever.

This book was originally written for the Modern Masters series published by Fontana and appeared shortly after Barthes's death. It analyses Barthes's achievements and makes available various Barthes for those who can find him useful, appealing, stimulating. The range of his work – of his moods and modes – is so broad that there is something for everyone here, but the key question is where can Barthes lead us, what does his appeal generate? For this new edition I have made only minor changes to the main text, both because I still stand by most of what I say here about Barthes and because too many interventions would risk creating an uneven text, where voices of youth and middle age struggled with each other. In addition to minor clarifications, I have inserted new bibliographical information, but above all I have added a final chapter on the fortunes of Barthes since his death and an argument about his particular value today.

Ithaca, New York
June 2001

Where references for quotations from Barthes's books are given in the text in the format (p. 154/136), the first number refers to the French edition and the second to the English translation listed in the Further reading section.

List of illustrations

The publisher and the author apologize for any errors or omissions in the above list. If contacted they will be pleased to rectify these at the earliest opportunity.

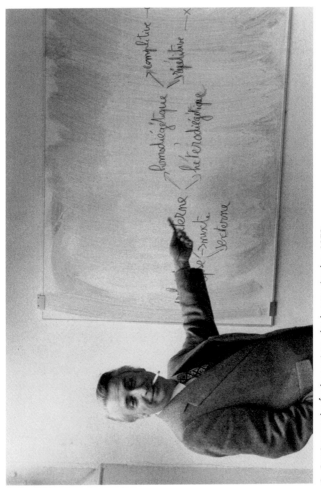

1. Seminar at the École pratique des hautes études, 1973.

Chapter 1
Man of parts

When Roland Barthes died in 1980 at the age of 65, he was a professor at the Collège de France, the highest position in the French academic system. He had become famous for incisive and irreverent analyses of French culture but was now himself a cultural institution. His lectures attracted huge, diverse crowds, from foreign tourists and retired schoolteachers to eminent academics; his reflections on aspects of daily life were featured in newspapers; his *Fragments d'un discours amoureux*, a 'rhetoric' of love, became a bestseller and was adapted for the stage.

Outside France, Barthes seemed to have succeeded Sartre as the leading French intellectual. His books were translated and widely read. A critical antagonist, Wayne Booth, called him 'the man who may well be the strongest influence on American criticism today', but his readership went far beyond the company of literary critics.[1] Barthes was a figure of international stature, a Modern Master. But what is he master of? What is he celebrated for?

In fact, Barthes is famous for contradictory reasons. To many, he is above all a structuralist, perhaps *the* structuralist, advocate of a systematic, scientific approach to cultural phenomena. The most prominent promoter of semiology, the science of signs, he also outlined a structuralist 'science of literature'.

To others, Barthes stands not for science but for pleasure: the pleasures of reading and the reader's right to read idiosyncratically, for what pleasure he or she can get. Against a literary criticism focused on authors – interested in recovering what authors thought or meant – Barthes champions the reader and promotes literature that gives the reader an active, creative role.

Third, Barthes is famous as a champion of the avant-garde. When French critics complained that the novels of Alain Robbe-Grillet and other practitioners of the *nouveau roman* were unreadable – jumbles of confusing descriptions without recognizable plots or engaging characters – Barthes not only praised these novels, linking his fortunes to theirs, but argued that the purposes of literature are best fulfilled precisely by 'unreadable' works that challenge our expectations. Against the 'readable' – works that conform to traditional codes and models of intelligibility – he set the 'writable' – experimental works that we don't yet know how to read but can only write and must in effect write as we read them.

Yet the writing for which this champion of the avant-garde is best known deals not with contemporary, experimental authors but with classic French writers, such as Racine and Balzac. His deepest love is 'French literature from Chateaubriand to Proust', and Proust seems his favourite author. One even suspects that his celebration of the avant-garde and apparent denigration of earlier literature was a brilliant strategy (conscious or unconscious) for creating a climate in which he might later return to these earlier authors and read them in new ways.

Finally, Barthes is famous as an agent of what he calls 'the death of the author', the elimination of this figure from the central place in literary studies and critical thinking. 'We now know', he wrote in 1968, 'that a text is not a line of words releasing a Single "theological" meaning (the "message" of an Author-God) but a multi-dimensional space in which a variety of writings, none of them original, blend and clash' (*Image,*

Music, Text, p. 146). He urged, with some effect, that we should study not authors but texts.

Yet this enemy of authors is himself pre-eminently an author, a writer whose varied products reveal a personal style and vision. Many of Barthes's works are idiosyncratic, falling outside established genres: *L'Empire des signes* combines touristic commentary on Japan with a reflection on signs in everyday life and their ethical implications; *Roland Barthes par Roland Barthes* is a strangely detached account of the life and works of one 'Roland Barthes' and evades the conventions of autobiography; *Fragments d'un discours amoureux* is specimens and formulae of lovers' talk rather than a study of love; and *La Chambre claire* must be called meditations on favourite photographs rather than an analysis of the art of photography. Peculiar yet compelling, these works are rightly celebrated as the imaginative products of an *author*, a master of French prose with a singular approach to experience.

Such is Roland Barthes, a figure of contradiction, with an intricate range of theories and stances that we must elucidate. How do we assess someone like this? When asked what Barthes is master of, one is tempted to reply, 'literary criticism'. (At the Collège de France he chose to be styled Professor of Literary Semiology.) Yet this scarcely covers his accomplishments, and his fame does not come from authoritative achievements in literary criticism. His influence is tied, rather, to the various projects he outlined and espoused, projects that helped to alter the way people think about a range of cultural objects, from literature, fashion, wrestling, and advertising, to notions of the Self, of history, and of nature.

One might, then, praise Barthes as a founder of disciplines, a proponent of methods; but this, too, proves somewhat awkward. Each time Barthes urged the merits of some new, ambitious project – a science of literature, a semiology, a science of contemporary myths, a narratology, a history of literary signification, a science of divisions, a typology of textual pleasure – he swiftly passed on to something else. Abandoning what he had set in motion, he often wrote wryly or disparagingly about his prior preoccupations. Barthes is a seminal thinker, but he tries to uproot his seedlings as they sprout. When his projects flourish, they do so without him and despite him.

This refusal to be tied down, this perpetual movement that aims not to correct errors but to evade the past, can be irritating to anyone who has read one of Barthes's works and been excited by its vision of things to be done. One is tempted to condemn Barthes's lack of perseverance and to praise instead those honest toilers in the vineyard who haven't shunned hard work for some alluring new prospect on the horizon. But Barthes interests us precisely because he is stimulating, and it is hard to separate what engages us in his works from his perpetual attempt to adopt new perspectives, to break with habitual perceptions. A lasting commitment to particular projects would have made Barthes a less productive thinker.

Recognizing this, Barthes's greatest admirers are inclined to praise precisely this desire for change, this unwillingness to be tied down, treating his writings not as analyses to be evaluated for their contributions to our understanding but as moments of a personal adventure. In effect, they cope with Barthes's contradictions by seeking a personality behind them, a personal intellectual style. They celebrate his restlessness rather than his structural analyses, his willingness to follow his interests and his pleasure rather than his achievements in this or that field.

In his inaugural lecture at the Collège de France, in which a new professor traditionally explains his approach to his subject, Barthes spoke not of developing a literary semiology or of extending knowledge but of *forgetting*: 'I undertake to let myself be borne on by that force of any living life: forgetting' (*Leçon*, p. 45/478). He proposed not to teach what he knew but to incarnate '*unlearning*, yielding to the unforeseeable modifications that forgetting imposes on the sedimented knowledge, culture and beliefs one has traversed.' For this movement of forgetting, this unlearning, he appropriated the Latin term for wisdom, *sapientia*, giving it his own definition: '*Sapientia*: no power, a little knowledge, a little wisdom, and as much flavour as possible' (*Leçon*, p. 46/478).

Barthes is always flavourful, perhaps especially when, in unexpected turns of phrase, he appears to make himself vulnerable. The idea that Barthes is essentially a flavoursome personality has gained authority because it suits two influential groups: Barthes's idolaters, for whom his every work is a 'Song of Roland', and journalists, who can discuss a personality more easily than a theorist. Barthes's 'unlearning', his abandonment of earlier positions, enabled the French press to describe Barthes's career on the banal model of the radical turned respectable: tiring of systems, principles, and politics, he had made his peace with society so as to enjoy its pleasures and to seek a personal fulfilment. The political stances and social critiques of the early and middle years were just a few of his many flavours, neglected by the mature Barthes, who shunned theories to cultivate his individuality. His 'doctrinaire' promotion of avant-garde literature could be treated as a youthful enthusiasm of one who later returned to the classics of French literature. The unlearning that moved Barthes beyond each position and each programme was seen as testimony to the ultimate worth of the French culture and French society he came to embrace. At the time of his death, this critic of capitalist society and its myths was hailed by politicians as a benign representative of French culture.

Readers who are not French may not be much concerned with what the media made of Barthes's conversions, or with his politics, or even with his precise relation to the avant-garde (in 1971 he claimed that his historical position was 'in the rearguard of the avant-garde' ['Réponses', p. 102]). Such questions must certainly remain subordinate to the primary task of this study, which is to elucidate Barthes's varied theoretical positions and contributions. But if one is to read Barthes at all, one must confront the fundamental question of how to take his ideas. Barthes's admirers repeatedly court the risk of trivializing his works by making them the expressions of a desire rather than arguments to be pondered, developed, or contested; and Barthes himself encourages this by mocking his past procedures. In *Barthes par Barthes*, for example, he considers some of the binary oppositions that played crucial roles in his earlier analyses, such as the distinctions between the *lisible* and the *scriptible* (the *readable* and the *writable*), *denotation* and *connotation, metaphor* and *metonymy*. A paragraph entitled 'Forgeries' calls these oppositions 'figures of production' that enable him to keep writing. 'The opposition is *struck* (like a coin), but one does not seek to *honour* it. Then what good is it? Quite simply, it serves *to say something*' (p. 96/92). And under the rubric 'La Machine de l'écriture' ('The Writing Machine'), he speaks of his enthusiasm for conceptual oppositions. 'Like a magician's wand, the concept, especially if it is coupled, *raises a* possibility of writing.' Here, he says, lies the possibility of saying something. 'Hence, the work proceeds by conceptual infatuations, successive enthusiasms, perishable manias [*engouements conceptuels, empourprements successifs, manies périssables*]' (p. 114/110).

Like so much of *Barthes par Barthes*, this wry self-mockery is seductive; one is encouraged by the older Barthes to feel superior to the younger Barthes, who mistakes his manias for valid concepts. But an intellectually curious reader must at least stop to ask whether this is the best way to read Barthes and whether Barthes's apparent demystification of his past work is not a remystification, a nimble and stylish evasion: given the difficulty of assessing one's past concepts, how tempting boldly to declare them infatuations or manifestations of an underlying desire to write that might link one with other authors. Barthes's mocking of his past may work to create a Barthesian myth. These passages of *Barthes par Barthes* could even be read as a form of showing off: like a young bicyclist shouting, 'Look, Ma! No hands!',

Barthes cries, 'Look, Ma! No Concepts!' A writer might well take pleasure in claiming that his writing was not sustained by significant theories but ran instead on perishable manias and that its fame rested not on its cognitive value but on the flair of its conceptual infatuations and successive enthusiasms.

Even if Barthes does take this view of his work – and his writing is too playful to authorize a definite conclusion – we need not join him in treating it as a series of infatuations that are less important than the fundamental desire they express. Though it would be a challenge to seek out a unifying, underlying desire, hoping thus to discover the 'true Barthes', it seems truer to Barthes – truer to the corpus of his writings and to the nature of his engagement with his times – to let him remain a chameleon, who participates with vigour and inventiveness in a series of very different projects. Instead of seeking a reductive unity, one should allow him to retain his vitality as a man of parts, engaged in a range of valuable general enterprises that may not have a common denominator.

If we must seek unity, if we still feel the need to sum up Barthes in a phrase, we might call him, as John Sturrock does in a useful essay, 'an incomparable enlivener of the literary mind.'[2] Better still, we might say what Barthes says of the writer in general: that he is 'a public experimenter' (*Essais critiques*, p. 10/xii). He tries out ideas and systems in public, for the public. An essay called 'What is Criticism?' develops this idea further. The critic's job, Barthes argues, is not to discover the secret meaning of a work – a truth of the past – but to construct intelligibility for our own time (*Essais critiques*, p. 257/260). To construct '*l'intelligible de notre temps*' is to develop conceptual frameworks for dealing with phenomena of the past and present. This, one can argue, is Barthes's fundamental activity, his most persistent concern. 'What has fascinated me all my life', he says in an interview, 'is the way people make their world intelligible' (*Le Grain de la voix*, p. 15/8). His writings attempt to show us how we do it and above all that we *are* doing it: the meanings that seem natural to us are cultural products, the result of

7

conceptual frameworks that are so familiar as to pass unnoticed. In challenging received opinion and proposing new perspectives, Barthes exposes habitual ways of making the world intelligible and works to modify them. To treat him as a public experimenter working to construct intelligibility for our time will help to account for much that is puzzling in his writings, while preserving their range of positions and perspectives. I shall do this by describing the different projects which Barthes explored.

First, though, a brief account of Barthes's life to provide points of reference for later discussions. As Barthes became famous, interviewers frequently asked about his life, and after some resistance he soon came to speak willingly, stressing all the while that 'any biography is a novel that dares not speak its name' ('Réponses', p. 89). Later I shall discuss some of the literary qualities of Barthes's biographical novel (as manifested, for example, in *Barthes par Barthes*). For the moment, all that concerns us is the plot and a few distinctive themes.

Barthes was born in 1915 to a middle-class, Protestant family. His father, a naval officer, was killed in action within a year, and Roland grew up with his mother and grandparents in Bayonne, a small city near the Atlantic coast in the southwestern corner of France. Discussions of his childhood in *Barthes par Barthes* (which is prefaced by the warning that 'All this must be considered as spoken by a character in a novel') emphasize music (his aunt was a piano teacher and Barthes played whenever the instrument was free), a background of bourgeois talk (the discourse of the provincial ladies who came to tea, for instance), and childhood sights and sounds recalled with a certain nostalgia. When Barthes was nine, he and his mother moved to Paris where she earned a meagre living as a bookbinder and his milieu was school (punctuated by vacations, which were spent in Bayonne). When Barthes was twelve, his mother had an affair with an artist in Bayonne and gave birth to a son, Barthes's half-brother, who lived with them for the rest of Barthes's life, though Barthes never mentions him. Barthes says little of his school years, but he was a good student, and on completion of his Baccalauréat in 1934 he planned to compete for a place at the École normale supérieure, where the very best students pursue their university education. But tuberculosis made its first appearance and he was sent to the Pyrenees for a cure. A year later he returned to Paris and worked toward a university degree in French, Latin, and Greek, devoting much time to performing classical plays with a group he helped to found.

When war began in 1939, Barthes, who had been exempted from military service, worked in lycées in Biarritz and Paris, but in 1941 a recurrence of tuberculosis put an end to this. He spent most of the next five years – roughly the period of the German occupation – in sanatoria in the Alps, where he led an ordered existence and read a great deal, emerging, he has said, as a Sartrean and a Marxist. After further convalescence in Paris he obtained posts teaching French abroad, first in Romania, then in Egypt, where he was introduced to modern linguistics by a colleague, A. J. Greimas.

Returning to France, he spent two years in the division of the government cultural service concerned with teaching abroad, but in 1952 he obtained a scholarship to work on a thesis in lexicology, on the vocabulary of social debate in the early 19th century. He made little progress on his thesis but published two works of literary criticism, *Le Degré zéro de l'écriture* (1953) and *Michelet par lui-même* (1954). Losing his scholarship, he worked for a publisher for a year while writing numerous articles, including many of the brief studies of contemporary culture to be published as *Mythologies* (1957). In 1955 friends helped him obtain another scholarship, this time for a sociological study of fashion, which eventually led to *Système de la mode* (1967). In 1960, after this scholarship had come to an end, he obtained a position at an institute on the margins of the university system, the École pratique des hautes études, where he became a regular teacher in 1962. Meanwhile, he was publishing the essays on the *nouveau roman* and other literary subjects that would be collected in *Essais critiques* (1964), pursuing the vision of a science of signs, articulated in *Éléments de sémiologie* (1964), and writing what proved to be a very controversial book, *Sur Racine* (1963).

Until 1965 Barthes was an active but marginal figure on the French intellectual scene, but then a Sorbonne professor, Raymond Picard, published *Nouvelle critique ou nouvelle imposture?* (New Criticism or New Charlatanism?), which attacked Barthes in particular and whose accusations, when taken up and rehashed in the French press, made Barthes the representative of everything that was radical, unsound, and irreverent in literary studies. Though Picard had objected above all to psychoanalytic formulations in Barthes's discussion of Racine, the fray swiftly became a general Quarrel of Ancients and Moderns that brought Barthes international notoriety. *Critique et vérité* (1966) answered Picard and proposed a structuralist 'science of literature', which Barthes pursued in subsequent articles on rhetoric and on narrative. Two other books related to the structuralist enterprise were published in ensuing years: *Sade/Fourier/Loyola* (1971), which studies this surprising trio of thinkers as founders of discursive systems, and *S/Z* (1970), Barthes's most extensive literary analysis. Meanwhile, a trip to Japan led to *L'Empire des signes* (1970), which Barthes claimed to enjoy writing more than any other book.

By the late 1960s Barthes was established as a Parisian eminence, along with Claude Lévi-Strauss, Michel Foucault, and Jacques Lacan. Greatly sought after, he at first accepted invitations to travel and lecture, enjoying the novelty of strange places and the opacity of foreign languages, but not the obligation of talk with new people. Never an enthusiastic performer like Foucault nor a lover of servile attention like Lacan, he swiftly grew tired of lecture tours, preferring to remain in the Parisian neighbourhood where he had spent most of his life, conducting his seminar at the École pratique des hautes études, and seeing friends.

At the height of his fame as a structuralist, Barthes published two books which greatly altered his reputation: *Le Plaisir du texte* (1973), whose

2. Structuralist fashions: Foucault, Lacan, Lévi-Strauss, and Barthes.

speculations on reading and pleasure made clear the ethical cast of his thought, and *Roland Barthes par Roland Barthes* (1975), whose graceful theoretization of ordinary experience and whose seductively self-deprecatory tone gave him a new status as a writer. In 1976 he was appointed to a chair at the Collège de France and in 1977 a week-long conference at Cérisy was devoted to his work. But Barthes refused to be professorial and immediately published *Fragments d'un discours amoureux* (1977), which embraced and explored the sentimental language of lovers. Nothing could have been more foreign to the concerns of the literary and theoretical avant-garde, but this unorthodox work proved extremely popular and helped make Barthes much more than an academic figure.

Confirmation of his status as a writer came in 1978 in a form that displeased him: a parodic *Le Roland-Barthes sans peine* (as in *French Without Tears*) which purported to teach, in 18 easy lessons, how to speak Roland-Barthes, a language which bears some resemblance to French. Barthes was now a stylist worthy of parody. Interviewers repeatedly asked him whether he would ever write a novel, and though he generally said no, he devoted several courses at the Collège de France to 'Preparation for the Novel', discussing writers' images of what they were trying to produce and their different ways of proceeding. In a Paris where psychoanalysis was the reigning intellectual fashion, Barthes seemed to have become the main promoter of traditional literary values and the principal non-psychoanalytical theorist of daily life. *La Chambre claire* (1980), in part a tribute to Barthes's mother, whose death in November 1977 had been a great blow, was a book on photography. The question of what he would do next, where his talents would take him, had become an intriguing mystery.

Then, in February 1980, coming out of a luncheon with socialist politicians and intellectuals, Barthes was knocked down by a laundry truck while crossing the street in front of the Collège de France. Though he recovered sufficiently to receive visitors, he died four weeks later. His death makes his career even more of a puzzle. It was not the tragic death of a scholar cut off in the midst of some great project, yet one could not say with assurance that Barthes's best work was behind him. Who knows what he might have gone on to do or what further experiments he might have performed?

In Barthes's life, as he recounts it, three factors are distinctive. First, there is the undramatic, nagging poverty of a middle-class family in reduced circumstances. 'His formative problem', Barthes says of Barthes, 'was doubtless money, not sex' (*Barthes par Barthes*, p. 50/45). He speaks not of misery but of financial embarrassment (*gêne*) – scrimping to buy schoolbooks and shoes – and relates this to his later love for the contrary of embarrassment, *ease* (pleasure, for Barthes, means ease rather than luxury).

Second, there is tuberculosis, which twice prevented him from taking the road to an academic career and, more important, imposed a special way of life. Barthes says that his body belongs to the world of Thomas Mann's *The Magic Mountain*, where the tubercular cure is indeed a way of life. Barthes grew accustomed to an ordered existence based on perpetual awareness of the body, a life of much talk but few events and of friendships made possible by continuing proximity.

Third, Barthes speaks euphemistically of a period of 'instability in his profession': from 1946 to 1962 he lived by short-term measures, with no clear direction or assured job. Later, when fame offered the opportunity of clear public and professional roles, he did not exploit his eminence as one might have expected. He speaks of a desire for flavour rather than power and seems indeed to have refrained from seeking the power he might have exercised – though his modesty has a certain power of its own.

One could relate these aspects of Barthes's life to his writings, deriving positions he took from aspects of his experience. Barthes himself sometimes attempts this, but such exercises are mostly unconvincing: each supposed cause – poverty, tuberculosis, instability – has numerous possible effects; the primary influence for each of Barthes's writings is rather the project in which it participates. He is marvellously inventive, but above all he has a nose for what is in the air and might be seized upon, developed, inventively installed as the ruling concept of a new

3. Fancy dress party at the sanatorium. Barthes is on the far right, dressed up as Barrès, member of the Académie française.

project. He has a superb sense of what will surprise but entice, what shocking paradox or contravention of habit might *take*; and thus the context within which or against which he writes is crucial. His is a special sort of mastery, suited to experimentation with the intelligibilities of our time.

Chapter 2
Literary historian

Barthes was always interested in history, for several reasons. First, history functions as the opposite of Nature. Cultures try to pass off as natural features of the human condition arrangements and practices that are in fact historical, the result of historical forces and interests. 'It is when history is denied', Barthes writes, 'that it is most unmistakably at work' (*Le Degré zéro de l'écriture*, p. 9/2). By showing when and how various practices came into being, historical study works to demystify the ideology of a culture, exposing its assumptions as ideology.

Second, Barthes values history for the strangeness of other epochs and what they can teach us about the present. Writing of the 17th-century moralist La Bruyère in *Essais critiques*, he suggests that we should 'underline all that separates his world from ours and all that this distance teaches us about ourselves; such is our enterprise here: let us discuss everything in La Bruyère which concerns us little or not at all: perhaps we shall then, at last, grasp the modern meaning of his work' (p. 223/223). History is interesting and valuable precisely for its otherness.

Third, history is useful because it can provide a story for making the present intelligible. That is what Barthes is seeking in his earliest work of criticism, *Le Degré zéro de l'écriture*. He sketches a history of writing (a history of the idea and institution of literature) that will situate contemporary literature and help one evaluate it. The greatest literary intellectual of the day, Jean-Paul Sartre, had published in 1948 an influential book, *What is Literature?*, which, in answering that question with a capsule history, had argued that to live up to its promise contemporary literature should turn away from aestheticism and linguistic play to social and political commitment. In a rejoinder that, interestingly, never mentions Sartre by name, Barthes provides an alternative story that leads to a different evaluation of contemporary literature.

In Sartre's lively and compelling account, French writers of the late 18th century were the last to find a proper and effective role, as they articulated for a powerful audience a progressive vision of the world that was also the vision of their own class. But after 1848, as the bourgeoisie developed an ideology to protect and justify its newly dominant role, writers – to put it simply – had either to yield to bourgeois ideology or else to renounce it and make themselves politically ineffective outcasts. The most 'advanced' literature thenceforth became a marginal activity without an appropriate audience. Flaubert and Mallarmé opted for a specialized, 'uncommitted' literature, and the surrealists of the 20th century chose what Sartre deems a futile and theoretical negation that eschews serious contact with the world.

Writers of his own generation, Sartre argues, with their intense experience of 'historicity' in the Second World War and the Resistance, could appreciate the importance of commitment and make literature what 'it essentially is, a taking of position'. 'Our job as writers is to represent the world and to bear witness to it.' For Sartre, poetry may play or experiment with language, but prose *uses* language: to name, to describe, to reveal.

> The function of a writer is to call a spade a spade [*appeler un chat un chat*]. If words are sick, it is up to us to cure them. Instead of that, many

writers live off this sickness. In many cases modern literature is a cancer of words ... In particular, there is nothing more deplorable than the literary practice called, I believe, poetic prose, which consists of using words for the obscure harmonics that resound about them, made up of vague senses in contradiction with the clear meaning.[3]

Writers should call things by their names in an efficient, transparent language.

Sartre's distinction between the unambiguous, transparent language of prose and the opaque, suggestive language of poetry implies that all the dealings with language which have characterized avant-garde literature since Flaubert ought to have been confined to the realm of poetry, and that the story of literature, from Flaubert and Mallarmé to surrealism and beyond, is one of error and decline. Barthes shares both Sartre's conviction that literature should have a vital relation to history and society and his sense that writers of the 18th century had an admirable situation (see his essay on Voltaire, 'The Last Happy Writer', in *Essais critiques*). He also accepts the claim, which makes more sense in France than elsewhere, that 1848 is the historical turning point (since Flaubert, Barthes says, literature has been a meditation on and encounter with language). What he rejects is the account of language and literature that makes self-conscious and modernist literature a deplorable, amoral aberration or a 'cancer of words'.[4]

Barthes starts, therefore, with a bold challenge to Sartre's notion that politically effective language is direct, transparent, literal.

Hébert [an activist of the French Revolution who edited a newssheet] never began a number of *Le Père Duchêne* without sprinkling it with *fuck* and *bugger*. These obscenities had no meaning but they had significance. How? They signified a whole revolutionary situation. Here is an example of a mode of writing whose function is no longer only communication or expression but the imposition of something beyond language, which is both history and the stand we take in it.

Le Degré zéro, p. 9/1

All writing contains signs, like Hébert's obscenities, that indicate a social mode, a relation to society. By its disposition on the page alone, a poem signals, 'I am poetry; do not read me as you would other language.' Literature has various ways of signifying 'I am literature,' and Barthes's book is a brief history of these 'signs of literature'. No prose is transparent, as Sartre would wish. Even the simplest language of novels – in Hemingway, for example, or Camus – signifies by indirection a relation to literature and to the world. A stripped-down language is not natural or neutral or transparent but a deliberate engagement with the institution of literature; its apparent rejection of literariness will itself become a new mode of literary writing, a recognizable *écriture*, as Barthes calls it. An author's *language* is something he inherits, and his *style* is a personal, perhaps subconscious network of verbal habits and obsessions, but his *mode of writing*, or *écriture*, is something he chooses, from the possibilities historically available. It is 'a way of conceiving literature', 'a social use of literary form'.

Barthes argues that from the 17th century to the mid-19th century French literature employed a single *écriture classique*, characterized primarily by confidence in the representational function of language. When Madame de Lafayette writes that Le Comte de Tende, on learning that his wife was pregnant by another man, 'thought everything it was natural to think in such circumstances', she shows the same sense of the function of writing as does Balzac nearly two centuries later when he writes that Eugène de Rastignac was 'one of those young men moulded for work by misfortune', or that Baron Hulot was 'one of those men whose eyes light up at the sight of a pretty woman'. This *écriture classique* is based on the assumption of a familiar, ordered, intelligible world to which literature refers. Here, writing is political by the way it connotes universality and intelligibility.

There are vast differences of thought and style within classical writing. Conversely, Barthes argues, though the differences in the thought of the near-contemporaries Balzac and Flaubert may be minor, there is a fundamental distinction between their *écritures*. After 1848, the argument goes, the *interested* character of bourgeois ideology became apparent. Where writers had previously assumed universality, now writing had to reflect upon itself as writing. To write was to contend self-consciously with literature. Barthes explains:

> These have been, *grosso modo*, the phases of the development: first an artisanal consciousness of literary fabrication, refined to the point of painful scruple (Flaubert); then, the heroic will to identify, in one and the same written matter, literature and the theory of literature (Mallarmé); then, the hope of somehow eluding literary tautology by ceaselessly postponing literature, by declaring that one is going to write, and by making this declaration into literature itself (Proust); then, the testing of literary good faith by deliberately, systematically, multiplying to infinity the meanings of the word without ever abiding by any one sense of what is signified (surrealism); finally, and inversely, rarefying these meanings to the point of trying to achieve a *Dasein* of literary language, a neutrality (though not an innocence) of writing: I am thinking here of the work of Robbe-Grillet.

> *Essais critiques*, pp. 106–7/97–8

This is an explanation from 1959. In 1953 in *Le Degré zéro*, however, Barthes was thinking not of Alain Robbe-Grillet but of Albert Camus, whose attempt at neutral, non-affective writing, Barthes called 'zero degree writing'. Sartre had seen Camus's *écriture blanche* as a refusal of commitment, but for Barthes, Camus's writing, like other examples of self-conscious literature since Flaubert, is historically engaged at another level: it struggles against 'literature' and its presumptions of meaning and order. Serious literature must question itself and the conventions by which culture orders the world; therein lies its radical potential. But 'no writing can be lastingly revolutionary', since each

Literary historian

4. Barthes at the time of the publication of *Le Degré zéro de l'écriture* (1953).

violation of the conventions of language and literature can ultimately be recuperated as a new mode of literature.

This first book of Barthes's, *Le Degré zéro*, is a strange work of criticism. It mentions few literary works and contains almost no examples – the only quotations are from an unnamed novel by communist intellectual Roger Garaudy. Later, in an article on literary history in *Sur Racine*, Barthes criticizes literary historians for having a historical method but neglecting the historical nature of their object of study. Here we seem to have just the opposite problem: Barthes emphasizes the historical character of his object – writing, or the literary function – but lacks a historical method. The idea of an *écriture classique* is scarcely fleshed out, and readers must envision examples for themselves. Barthes does not analyse or demonstrate. He does not even *answer* Sartre (Sartre's book is mentioned nowhere in the text).[5] Rather, he seems to be experimenting with Sartre's story of literature: modifying it so as to produce a different conception of literary history and evaluation of post-Flaubertian writing.

This brief foray into literary history does three things. First, it asserts the 'political and historical engagement of literary language'. The political significance of writing is not simply a matter of political content or of an author's overt political commitment but also of the work's engagement with a culture's literary ordering of the world. Barthes does not, unfortunately, show in detailed analyses how one might determine the political implications of experimental writing, but he suggests that literature's exploration of language and critique of inherited codes releases a valuable utopian and interrogative impulse. What he shows most convincingly is that since even political tracts work by indirection, it is no simple matter to evaluate the political significance of writing.

Second, *Le Degré zéro* established a general historical narrative that facilitates thinking about literature. Later, Barthes would complicate the story he sets up here of an unself-conscious and representational literature replaced, after 1848, by a self-conscious, problematical and experimental literature. In *S/Z* he distinguishes between the *readerly* (*lisible*) and the *writerly* (*scriptible*): the readerly is what we know how to read and thus has a certain transparency; the writerly is self-conscious and resistant to reading. This new historical distinction is more explicitly tied to reading practices of the present than to historical events, but it has its germ in the distinction between classic and modern *écritures* by which Barthes first tried to make the present intelligible.

Finally, in focusing on the signs of literature – the way writing connotes a literary mode – Barthes brings to our attention and to his a diffuse but powerful second level of meaning, which he will go on to study in myriad guises. This second-order signification he calls 'myth', and it is as mythologist that Barthes first came into his own.

Chapter 3
Mythologist

Between 1954 and 1956, Barthes wrote brief monthly feature articles called 'Mythology of the Month' for *Les Lettres nouvelles.* 'I resented seeing Nature and History confused at every turn in accounts of contemporary life,' he reports, and in discussing aspects of mass culture he sought to analyse the social stereotypes passed off as natural, unmasking 'what-goes-without-saying' as an ideological imposition. *Mythologies*, which collects these articles with a long concluding essay called 'Myth Today', is Barthes's most amusing and accessible book, but it poses one formidable difficulty: what does Barthes mean by 'myth'?

In many cases, as he reveals the ideological implications of what seems natural, 'myth' means a delusion to be exposed. A good example is an exposition of photographs entitled 'The Family of Man' (in French, '*La Grande famille des hommes*') 'whose aim', Barthes writes, 'was to show the universality of human actions in the daily life of all the countries of the world,' to suggest that 'birth, death, work, knowledge, play, always impose the same types of behaviour,' and thus to portray humanity in all its variety as one large family (p. 173/100). By presenting the human diversity it celebrates as family variations of feature and physiognomy, this myth masks the radically different social and economic conditions under which people are born, work, and die. 'Everything here . . . aims to suppress the determining weight of history' by placing a common Human Nature beneath the superficial differences of human appearances, institutions, and circumstances. Progressive thought, Barthes argues, 'must always remember to reverse the terms of this very old imposture, and constantly to scrape away at Nature, its "laws" and its "limits", in order to uncover History there and finally to establish Nature itself as historical' (p. 175/101).

Each of the photographs in the exhibition represents a human scene; gathered together in this fashion, they acquire the second-order, mythical meaning that Barthes wishes to expose. Other objects and practices, even the most utilitarian, function the same way, endowed with second-order meaning by social usage. Wine, for example, is not just one drink among others in France, but 'a totem-drink, corresponding to the milk of the Dutch cow or the tea ceremoniously taken by the British Royal Family'. It is 'the foundation of a collective morality'. For the French, 'to believe in wine is a coercive collective act', and drinking wine a ritual of social integration (pp. 75–6/58–9). In generating mythical meaning, cultures seek to make their own norms seem facts of nature.

> The whole of France is steeped in this anonymous ideology: our press, our films, our pulp literature, our rituals, our Justice, our diplomacy, our conversation, our remarks about the weather, a murder trial, a touching wedding, the cuisine we dream of, the garments we wear, everything in everyday life, is dependent upon the representation which the bourgeoisie *has and makes us have* of the relations between man and the world. . . . bourgeois norms are experienced as the self-evident laws of a natural order.
>
> pp. 127–8/140

But if 'everything in everyday life' becomes the mythologist's domain, myths are not simply delusions to be exposed, like the myth of the Great Family of Man. Though the 'excellence of wine' is a myth, it is not exactly a delusion. Barthes notes the mythologist's dilemma: 'wine is objectively good, and *at the same time*, the goodness of wine is a myth'

(p. 246/158). The mythologist is concerned with the image of wine – not its properties and effects but the second-order meanings attached to it by social convention. Beginning with myth as delusion, Barthes soon comes to emphasize that myth is a form of communication, a 'language', a system of second-order meaning, similar to the *écriture* discussed in his previous book. Hébert's obscenities, for example, have a first order meaning as linguistic signs, but far more important is their mythical meaning: obscenity as a sign of revolution. *Mythologies* offers another example: when a student opens his Latin grammar and finds a sentence from Aesop about the lion demanding the largest portion, *quia ego nominor leo* (because my name is lion), he sees that the first-order linguistic meaning is much less important than the second-order meaning the sentence conveys, of 'I am a grammatical example illustrating the agreement of the predicate' (p. 201/116). In culture, one might say, everything exemplifies: a loaf of French bread signifies Frenchness.

Le Degré zéro, as Barthes now emphasizes, was not only an exercise in literary history but 'a mythology of literary language. There I defined writing as the signifier of the literary myth, that is, a form already full of [linguistic] meaning which receives from the era's concept of Literature a new meaning' (*Mythologies*, p. 221/134). Whatever its linguistic content, writing signifies an attitude towards literary form and thus towards meaning and order; it promotes a myth of literature and through this myth it acquires a role in the world. By exploring the ideological implications of a range of less exalted activities, *Mythologies* helps to suggest how literary myths could have social import.

Barthes's targets in these essays are varied. Sometimes he turns his attention to products invested with mythical signification by advertising campaigns. He writes about the latest model Citroën, about the image of plastic emerging in the 1950s, or about the peculiar dramatic scenarios starring soap powders and cleaning liquids: purifying liquids 'kill' dirt and germs, while soap powders are penetrating agents that lift out dirt, liberating the object from a subtle and elusive enemy. 'To say that Omo cleans in depth is to assume that linen is deep, which no one had previously thought' (p. 39/37). Barthes discusses the idea of the world enshrined in the *Guide bleu*, the media's treatment of royalty, flying saucers, Einstein's brain, and other mythical objects. Writing out meanings that are taken for granted, sarcastically intensifying them or speculating about their implications, he will then conclude with a laconic punchline, pulling us out of the myth by mentioning some political or economic interest at stake.

Barthes's most impressive analysis of second-order cultural meaning comes in the opening essay of *Mythologies*, 'The World of Wrestling'. To bring out the categories and distinctions through which culture gives meaning to behaviour, one can compare two physically similar activities such as wrestling and boxing, which show that there must indeed be different conventions at work to generate different mythical meanings. We could imagine a culture in which the two sports shared a single myth and were watched in the same way, but in our culture there is clearly a difference in ethos that requires explanation. Why does one bet on boxing but not on wrestling? Why would it be odd for a boxer to cry out and writhe in agony, as wrestlers do? Why are rules constantly broken in wrestling but not in boxing? These differences are explained by a complex set of cultural conventions that make wrestling a spectacle rather than a contest.

Boxing, Barthes says, is a Jansenist sport based on the demonstration of excellence: interest is directed toward the final outcome and visible suffering would be read only as sign of an imminent defeat. Wrestling, on the other hand, is drama in which each moment must be immediately intelligible as spectacle; the wrestlers themselves are physical caricatures cast in moral roles, and the outcome is of interest only for that reason – for its dramatic signification. Thus, while in boxing rules are external to the match, designating limits beyond which it must not go, in wrestling they are very much within it, as conventions that increase the range of meanings that can be produced. Rules exist to be violated, so that the 'bastard' may be more violently characterized and the audience engaged in revengeful fury. They are broken visibly (though the referee's back may be turned): a violation hidden from the audience would be pointless. Suffering must be exaggerated; and indeed, as Barthes shows, particular notions of intelligibility and of justice are the major factors that separate wrestling from boxing and make it the grandiloquent and fundamentally reassuring spectacle it is.

Wrestling attracts Barthes for a number of reasons: it is a popular rather than a bourgeois pastime; it prefers scene to narrative, revelling in theatrical signifying gestures; and it is unabashedly artificial, not only in its signs of pain, anger, and distress but even in its outcome: no one would be shocked to learn that matches are fixed. Later, in his mythology of the Orient, *L'Empire des signes*, Barthes praises daily life in Japan for its artifice – its elaborate etiquette, its preference for surface over depth, its refusal, at least in the eyes of a Westerner, to try to ground its practices in Nature. 'If there is a "health" of language, it is the arbitrariness of the sign that is its foundation. What is sickening in myth is the resort to a false Nature' (*Mythologies*, p. 212/126).

Myth always has an 'alibi' ready: its practitioners can always deny that second-order meaning is involved, claiming they wear certain clothes for comfort or for durability, not for meaning. But mythical meanings work on despite all denials. In a more political example, Barthes cites a cover of the magazine *Paris-Match* depicting a young black soldier in French uniform giving the military salute, his eyes fixed on the national flag. This is the first level of signification: shapes and colours are interpreted as a black soldier in French uniform. 'But naive or not,' Barthes writes, 'I see very well what it signifies to me: that France is a great empire, that all her sons, without any colour discrimination, serve faithfully under her flag, and that there is no better answer to the detractors of an alleged colonialism than the zeal this young black shows in serving his so-called oppressors' (p. 201/116). The fact that there are indeed black soldiers in the French army gives the photograph a certain naturalness or innocence; its defenders could claim that it is simply a picture of a black soldier and nothing more, just as the wearers of fur coats maintain that they are only interested in keeping warm. The bad faith of this persistent alibi is one of the things Barthes finds most objectionable in myth.

His dislike is no doubt intensified by an awkward fact: the mythologist puts himself in complicity with what he attacks, as he articulates what goes without saying, spelling out mythical meaning. When Barthes calls the modern automobile 'the exact equivalent of the great Gothic cathedrals: I mean the supreme creation of an era; conceived with passion by unknown artists; and consumed in image if not in usage by a whole population which appropriates them as a purely magical object' (p. 150/88), he mounts a critique of our era but also contributes to the myth. In 1971 Barthes noted that analysing and denouncing myths was not enough: instead of trying to promote a healthier use of signs, one must try to destroy the sign itself (*Image, Music, Text*, p. 167). Whether or not this would be more efficacious, we can certainly infer from what has happened since the publication of *Mythologies* that demystification does not eliminate myth but, paradoxically, gives it a greater freedom. Once upon a time, one could embarrass politicians by accusing them of working to promote an image of themselves, but as demystification became more frequent, embarrassment diminished, and now a candidate's aides publicly discuss how they are attempting to change their master's image. Or again, when feature articles identify particular objects as signs of a certain lifestyle, this does not destroy their mythical efficacy but generally makes them more desirable. Barthes describes how this cultural mechanism functions in literature: the most resolutely anti-literary movement does not destroy literature but becomes in turn a new school of literature. The same mechanism is at work in the non-literary realm. Exposure of the ways a president manipulates events to create an image leads not to the destruction of the image but to new possibilities of second-order meaning: a presidential act or decision can then be taken not as a sign of policy, nor even as a contribution to his image, but as a sign that he is concerned with his image. Myth is protean, and perhaps indomitable.

Barthes's *Mythologies* stands at the beginning of a tradition of demystification, which he hoped would have political results. Analysing myths, he argued in 1953, 'is the only effective way for an intellectual to take political action.'[6] Though he later favoured replacing the irony or sarcasm of the mythologist with a thorough critique of the sign, in fact his works of the 1970s retain the mythologist's fascination with second-order meanings; and the myths of everyday life become a resource for writing rather than an occasion for taking political positions. As he remarked in an interview, 'In daily life, I feel for everything I see and hear a sort of curiosity, almost an intellectual affection, which is on the order of the novelistic' (*Le Grain de la voix*, p. 192/203).

The novelistic, for Barthes, is the novel minus story and characters: fragments of astute observation, details of the world as bearers of second-order meaning. The novelistic eye for detail that enlivens *Mythologies* appears later in the constructions of *Fragments d'un discours amoureux*, which portrays the myth of love – the discourse of lovers as repertoire of cultural stereotypes – and in the reflections on daily life in *Barthes par Barthes*. There he notes, for example, that even the weather is charged with second-order, mythical meaning: talking about the weather with the woman at the bakery, he remarks, 'and the light is so beautiful' – but she makes no reply, and he realizes that nothing is more cultural than the weather: 'I realize that *seeing the light* relates to a class sensibility; or rather, since there are "picturesque" lights that are certainly enjoyed by the woman at the bakery, what is socially marked is the "vague", view, the view without contours, without object, *without figuration*, the view of a transparency' (p. 178/176). One might say that the light is objectively beautiful, but the beauty of the light is a myth, entangled with the conventions of a cultural group. This is the discovery of the mythologist: that the most 'natural' remark about the world depends on cultural codes. As Pascal put it, if custom is a second nature, as it manifestly is in these cultures that would pass as natural, then perhaps Nature is only a second custom.

Chapter 4
Critic

Despite his many unorthodox activities, Barthes devoted considerable time to the critic's traditional task of interpreting and evaluating writers' achievements. He wrote many prefaces and introductions, to modern, experimental writings and to French classics, but his most important work as a critic falls into two categories: the books in which he analyses the entire oeuvre of a writer of the past – Michelet, Racine, Sade – and the articles in which he champions an avant-garde writer – Brecht, Robbe-Grillet, Sollers – and energetically promotes a particular conception of literature's contemporary mission.

Barthes was always a master of surprise, and his early book on Michelet displays something of this talent. *Le Degré zéro* celebrates self-conscious, modernist literary projects, and one imagines its author turning next to Camus or to Blanchot – contemporaries attempting to practise the anti-literary literature he had described. Instead he took up Jules Michelet, a prolific, popular historian of the early 19th century, a colourful writer and ardent patriot, admirer of the French Revolution and of a picturesque, mysterious Middle Ages, which he chronicled in numerous volumes of imaginative history. Michelet's writing shows none of the self-conscious restraint Barthes claims to admire, but he seems to be one of Barthes's great loves, along with Proust and Sade. While in the sanatorium, Barthes reports, he read all Michelet's works – a herculean task – and copied out all the sentences that pleased him or repeated something striking. 'In arranging these cards, a bit as one might amuse oneself with a deck of playing cards, I couldn't avoid coming up with an account of themes' ('Réponses', p. 94).

This account became *Michelet par lui-même* (1954), a book concerned with what Barthes calls *style* in *Le Degré zéro*: 'the organized network of obsessions' manifested in Michelet's imaginative world. He dismisses Michelet's ideas in favour of what he calls an 'existential thematics', his writing's intense investment in various substances and qualities: blood, warmth, dryness, fecundity, smoothness, liquefaction (a famous passage on the French Revolution contrasts the dryness and sterility of Robespierre with the vital warmth of the mob). 'Strip Michelet of his existential thematics', Barthes writes, 'and there remains only a petit-bourgeois', unworthy of attention (p. 88/95).

Where *Le Degré zéro* stressed the ideological implications of literary form, *Michelet* turns away from such questions to describe a universe of contrasting qualities and substances. Barthes thus produced a work that was closely in touch with current developments in French criticism, where a model for discussing the importance of material substances for poetic and non-poetic thinking had emerged from Gaston Bachelard's 'psychoanalysis' of the four elements, earth, air, fire, and water. Barthes claimed not to have read Bachelard, which is quite possible; but Barthes's work was seen as a contribution to the growing body of phenomenological criticism which treated literary works not as artefacts to be analysed but as manifestations of consciousness: a consciousness or experience of the world in which readers are invited to participate. Georges Poulet's *Études sur le temps humain* (1950) and *La Distance intérieure* (1952) had recently appeared; Jean Starobinski had just published *Montesquieu par lui-même* (1953) in the series for which Barthes was writing, and the following year another critic of the so-called 'Geneva School' of phenomenological critics, Albert Béguin, published two further volumes in this collection (on Pascal and

Notes

in bed . . .

Reversal: of scholarly origin, the note follows the various twists and turns of movement.

. . . outside . . .

. . . or at a desk

5. Notes.

Bernanos). Most important, perhaps, Jean-Pierre Richard's *Littérature et sensation*, which appeared at the same time, argued explicitly for what seems to be the assumption of Barthes's *Michelet*: 'it is in sensation that everything begins; flesh, objects, moods, compose for the self a primal space,' and it is here, in physical affect, that literary forms, themes, and images are born.

Michelet par lui-même seemed part of the new wave of phenomenological criticism, but in the light of Barthes's later work two things are striking. First, Barthes's method enables him to make Michelet's writing a series of spectacular fragments, associating the interest of writing not with continuity, development, structure – all undeniable qualities of Michelet's work as a historian – but with the pleasure of textual fragments, the pleasure readers can get from odd sentences and their images. Second, this textual pleasure, which leads Barthes to write around and about these texts, is linked to the body. A link is posited between writing and corporeal experiences of space and substance.

Later, Barthes would dwell particularly upon the relation between his own writing and bodily experiences, as if corporeal sensation could serve as origin or ground.[7] Although phenomenological criticism is explicitly concerned with the experience or *appearance* of phenomena (the world as it appears to consciousness), it seems to lead its practitioners to treat the corporeal experience they come to posit as something of a natural foundation. The most highly wrought cultural artifacts are traced back to elementary, pre-reflective sensation, which serves as a natural origin. Barthes's most incisive and productive work combats the mystification that translates culture into nature; and in considering his later works, which strategically ground writing in the body, we shall have to ask whether this is not a mystification of the same genre. *Michelet par lui-même*, apparently so out of keeping with Barthes's literary and political commitments of 1954, explores positions that will reappear.

Sur Racine resembles *Michelet* in its concentration on an imaginative world, but it is neither a fascinated writing out of sentences and fragments, as *Michelet* is, nor a phenomenological description focused on substance and qualities. Less interested in Racine's language and imagination than in the tragic universe that imprisons his characters, Barthes undertakes what he calls an 'anthropology of Racinean man' in a 'mildly psychoanalytic language'. Asking what sort of creature inhabits this tragic universe, he superposes the plays, treating them as variant realizations of the system of Racinean tragedy and attempting to identify the fundamental relations that produce its situations and its characters. He puts special emphasis on a combination of three relations, of authority, of rivalry, and of love, that are found in the myth of the primal horde, as told by Freud and others: after banding together to kill the father who has dominated them and prevented them from taking wives, the sons eventually create a social order (and incest taboo) to control their rivalry. 'This story, even if it is a fiction, is the whole of Racine's theatre' (p. 20/8). Put together all the plays to form a single tragedy and 'you discover the figures and the actions of this primeval horde. . . . The Racinean theatre finds its coherence only on the level of this ancient fable.' Beneath the surface, 'the archaic bedrock is there, close at hand,' and the characters receive their qualities from their place in this general configuration of forces.

In *Essais critiques* Barthes claims that the writer produces 'presumptions of meaning, forms, as it were, and it is the world which fills them' (p. 9/ xi). This would make criticism the art of filling; or perhaps we should say, in keeping with Barthes's notion of the writer as public experimenter, that the critic experiments with fillings, trying out on an author or a work the languages and contexts that are available. This is how Barthes presents *Sur Racine*: 'let us try out on Racine, in virtue of his very silence, all the languages our century suggests' (p. 12/x). Racine is 'silent' because he created forms that presume but do not determine meaning. His plays are 'an empty site eternally open to signification', and if he is the greatest French author, 'his genius is to be located in none of the

Critic

virtues that have successively made his fortune but rather in an unrivalled art of availability, which permits him to remain eternally within the field of any critical language' (p. 11/ix).

To call the great French classic 'an empty site' is a calculated piece of rudeness, as is the decision to try out the language of psychoanalysis on this author traditionally regarded as the acme of purity, decorum, and conscious artifice. The result is a provocative, hybrid reading where three approaches Barthes is interested in exploring are uneasily combined: the phenomenological description of an imaginative universe, the structural analysis of a system, and the use of a contemporary 'language' to produce new thematic interpretations of individual works. As it happens, the description of an imaginative world loses much of its phenomenological character when the account of the 'archaic bedrock' becomes structural and seeks not qualities but differences and relations; and the structuralist attempt to treat the plays as the products of a system of formal rules is deflected by the attempt to produce surprising thematic readings of each play by drawing upon the language of myth and psychoanalysis. *Sur Racine* is a provocative book from which every reader takes a range of ideas about Racine, and it showed a wide public that works of literary criticism (or at least products of *la nouvelle critique*, as theoretically inspired criticism came to be called) could be fascinating reading, but it is not a model to which Barthes or others would return.

In *Sade/Fourier/Loyola*, where Barthes again treats a writer's work as a system, two aspects of *Sur Racine* are accentuated and transformed. The idea, taken from linguistics, that one could produce a 'grammar' of an author's work, discovering its basic elements and their rules of combination, had seemed a relatively unimportant manifestation of the reductive impulse behind *Sur Racine*. In *Sade/Fourier/Loyola* the linguistic analogy comes fully into its own: these three writers are treated as 'logothetes', or creators of special 'languages'. Sade's exhaustive narratives of sexual adventures, Fourier's invention of a utopian society, and Loyola's prescriptions for spiritual exercises all display the same proclivity to distinguish, order, and classify; they elaborate systems which, like languages, generate signification in the domain they articulate.

'There is an erotic grammar in Sade', Barthes writes, '(a porno-grammar) – with its erotemes and rules of combination' (p. 169/165), for Sadian eroticism seeks to 'combine according to precise rules the specific actions of vice, so as to make from these series and groups of actions a new "language", no longer spoken but acted, a language of crime, or a new code of love, as elaborate as the code of courtly love' (p. 32/27). The minimal unit of the erotic code is the *posture*, 'the smallest possible combination, since it unites only an action and its bodily point of application'. In addition to sexual poses, there are various 'operators' such as family ties, social rank, and physiological variables. Postures can be combined to form 'operations' or composite erotic tableaux, and when operations are given a temporal development, they become 'episodes'. 'All these units,' Barthes continues,

> are subject to rules of combination or composition. These rules would easily permit a formalization of the erotic language analogous to the 'tree structures' used by linguists. . . . In the Sadean grammar there are two principal rules; these are, as it were, regular procedures by which the narrator mobilizes the units of his 'lexicon' (postures, figures, episodes). The first is a rule of exhaustivity: in an 'operation' the greatest possible number of postures should be accomplished simultaneously. . . . The second is a rule of reciprocity . . . all functions can be exchanged, everyone can and should be in turn agent and victim, flagellator and flagellated, coprophagist and coprophagee, etc. This rule is central, first because it makes Sadean eroticism truly a formal language, in which there are only classes of actions and not groups of individuals, which greatly simplifies the grammar, and second because it prevents us from dividing Sadean society according to sexual roles.
>
> pp. 34–5/29–30

In addition to discovering a fuller critical role for the linguistic model, *Sade/Fourier/Loyola* transforms a second aspect of *Sur Racine*. There, Barthes's application of sexual or psychoanalytic language to Racine and his characters might have seemed an attempt to shock a French public instilled with a belief in Racinean decorum, but in *Sade/Fourier/Loyola* Barthes shows that he is especially interested in the effects produced by bringing discordant languages into contact, as when the technical terms of linguistics grate against the violent content of Sade's sexual vision. This is not mockery of cultural monuments so much as an exploration of the effects of combining languages.[8]

Sade/Fourier/Loyola, like *Michelet* and *Sur Racine*, shows that trying out one's century's languages on an author is not an attempt to make his works 'relevant' by showing that they have something to say about current problems. That would be a thematic enterprise, emphasizing Racine's psychology of love or Michelet's political views. On the contrary, Barthes's trying out of contemporary languages generally accentuates the strangeness of the writings he treats – Michelet's obsessions, Racine's claustrophobic universe, Sade, Fourier, and Loyola's classifying manias. None of these last three, he writes, 'is bearable [*respirable*]; each makes pleasure, happiness, communication, dependent upon an inflexible order or, worse still, on a system of combinations' (p. 7/3). Barthes's writing about these oeuvres does not discover relevant themes but seeks instead to 'unglue the text' from its vision and purpose – 'socialism, faith, evil', in Fourier, Loyola, and Sade, respectively – and *steal* its language, 'to fragment the old text of culture, knowledge, literature, and scatter its features in unrecognizable formulations, as one disguises stolen goods' (p. 15/10). An unusual programme for criticism, certainly; one which sees interest in strangeness rather than familiarity and finds pleasure in fragments. Barthes is strikingly unconcerned to describe the contours or construction of individual works. In stealing the language of writers of the past, he seeks to elucidate practices of writing and their implications for meaning and order rather than to interpret and evaluate finished works.

This is also apparent in Barthes's other main activity as critic, his promotion of certain avant-garde literary practices His first cause is a theatrical *écriture*, a social use of literary form he discovered in Brecht in the 1950s. At university Barthes had founded a group for the performance of Greek plays, and after the war he helped to establish the magazine *Théâtre populaire*, which attacked commercial drama of the day and argued for a theatre that would treat social and political issues. Sartre had succeeded in creating political drama, but Barthes sought to imagine a political theatre that was not wedded to a simplistic view of language and form. In 1954, when Brecht brought his Berliner Ensemble troupe to Paris, Barthes found his man. He was, he reports, 'literally set on fire' (*incendié*) by the performance of *Mother Courage* and by a passage from Brecht's writing on the theatre printed in the programme (*Le Grain de la voix*, p. 212/225). 'Brecht is still extremely important for me,' he wrote in 1971, 'the more so since he is not fashionable and has not yet succeeded in becoming part of the avant-garde one takes for granted. What makes him exemplary for me is properly speaking neither his Marxism nor his aesthetic (although both are very important) but the conjunction of the two: namely of Marxist analysis and thinking about meaning. He was a Marxist who had reflected upon *effects of the sign*: a very rare thing' ('Réponses', p. 95).

Brecht provided the new dramatic practice Barthes had been looking for and a theoretical perspective that helped him explain what was wrong with traditional Western theatre. Even when they do not mention Brecht, Barthes's writings on drama through the years reflect Brecht's notion of *Verfremdung*, or alienation, and his fundamental proposition that effective theatre requires not empathetic identification with major characters but a critical distance that enables us to judge and comprehend their situation. In Brecht's *Mother Courage*, Barthes argues, 'the point is to show those who believe in the fatality of war, like Mother Courage, that war is precisely a human phenomenon, not a fatality . . . because we *see* Mother Courage blind, we *see* what she does not see. . . . We understand, in the grip of this dramatic obviousness which is the most immediate kind of persuasion, that Mother Courage blind is the victim of what she does not see, which is a remediable evil' (*Essais critiques*, pp. 48–9/334).

Another example: the audience's identification with Marlon Brando in Elia Kazan's *On the Waterfront* weakens the political force of this film, for although the corrupt union is defeated and the bosses are presented satirically, at the end we join Brando as he gives himself over to the employers and the system. Barthes writes:

> Here or never is a case where we should apply the method of demystification Brecht proposes and examine the consequences of our identification with the film's leading character . . . it is the *participational* nature of this scene which objectively makes it an episode of mystification. . . . Now it is precisely against the danger of such mechanisms that Brecht proposed his method of alienation. Brecht would have asked Brando to *show* his naïvete, to make us understand that, despite the sympathy we may have for his misfortunes, it is even more important to perceive their causes and their remedies.
>
> *Mythologies*, pp. 68–9/*The Eiffel Tower*, pp. 40–1

Barthes finds three major lessons in Brecht. First, Brecht sees the theatre (and, by implication, literature) in cognitive rather than emotive terms and thus emphasizes the mechanisms of signification. He challenges the notion of a unified spectacle, showing Barthes that 'codes of expression can be detached from one another, pulled free from the sticky organicism in which they are held by the Western theatre' (*Image, Music, Text*, p. 175). 'The responsibility of dramatic art is not so much to express reality as to signify it' (*Essais critiques*, p. 87/74). Sets, costumes, gestures, and staging should not try to be 'naturally expressive'. Better to signify an army with a few banners than to express it with a cast of thousands.

Second, theatre should exploit the arbitrariness of the sign, drawing attention to its own artifice rather than attempting to conceal it. This is Barthes's version of Brecht's principle of *Verfremdung*. Actors and actresses performing Racine should speak their lines as verse instead of attempting to make this formal and highly ordered language seem the natural expression of psychological states. Barthes cites with approval Brecht's idea that the actor should speak his part not as if he were living it and improvising it but 'like a quotation'. He admires a range of theatrical practices that are unabashedly artificial, from the spectacles of professional wrestling described in *Mythologies* to the Kabuki theatre and Bunraku puppet theatre of Japan, celebrated in *L'Empire des signes*. There is, he suggests, a demystificatory political potential in any dramaturgy that abandons a theatre of character and inner psychological states for a theatre of situations and surfaces. Actors, playwrights, and producers should heed Barthes's favourite slogan: *Larvatus prodeo* (I advance pointing to my mask).

Third, 'Brecht *affirmed* meaning but did not *fill* it in' (*Essais critiques*, p. 260/263). His techniques of estrangement were designed to produce 'a theatre of consciousness, not of action', or, more precisely, a theatre of '*consciousness of unconsciousness*, consciousness of the unconsciousness prevailing on stage – that is Brecht's theatre', bringing the audience to an awareness of problems but not propagandistically advocating a solution. Even if this were not true of Brecht's theatre, it is the programme Barthes advocates for literature, which should not try to tell us what things mean but call attention to the way meaning is produced. Barthes articulates this view, when writing on the theatre, in language sustained by some fundamental contrasts: surface versus depth, outside versus inside, lightness versus heaviness, critical distance versus empathetic identification, mask versus character, sign versus reality, discontinuity versus continuity, emptiness or ambiguity versus

41

fullness of meaning, artificiality versus naturalness. Can political efficacy have a light touch? That is the possibility Brecht seems to offer.

At the same time that he was 'set on fire' by Brecht, Barthes became a fervent supporter of novelist Alain Robbe-Grillet, to whom four of the pieces in *Essais critiques* are devoted. 'What has fascinated me all my life', Barthes affirms, 'is the way mankind makes its world intelligible.' Robbe-Grillet's novels explore this process by attempting a heroic but impossible elimination of meaning, thus bringing to our attention the ways we are accustomed to make things intelligible. In *Le Degré zéro* Barthes had argued that the adoption of an *écriture* – 'a way of conceiving literature', 'a social use of literary form' – has political implications and that formal experimentation may be a mode of commitment, as in the attempts to write anti-literary literature and achieve writing degree zero. Camus's revolt against literature did not carry very far, for he made the meaninglessness of the world a *theme*; things still had meaning: they signified 'absurdity', as readers and critics swiftly came to call it. Robbe-Grillet seemed to Barthes to be attempting something more radical, in trying to empty or suspend meaning by frustrating our assumptions about intelligibility and blocking our regular interpretative moves. His detailed, gratuitous descriptions, empty characters and uncertain plots seemed at first unreadable, that is, unintelligible according to traditional assumptions about novels and about the world; but Barthes saw in his 'rejection of story, anecdote, psychology of motivation, and signification of objects' a powerful questioning of our ordering of experience.

> Since ... things are buried under the assorted meanings with which men, through sensibilities, through poetry, through different uses, have impregnated the name of each object, the novelist's labour is in a sense cathartic: he purges things of the undue meaning men ceaselessly deposit upon them. How? Obviously by description. Robbe-Grillet thus produces descriptions of objects sufficiently geometrical to discourage

any induction of poetic meaning and sufficiently detailed to break the
fascination of the narrative.

Essais critiques, p. 199/198

This account stresses two things. First, Barthes sees Robbe-Grillet's
writings, with their descriptions that block the induction of meaning, as
texts that are all surface. Depth and interiority have traditionally been
the domain of the novel, which tries to delve deep into characters and
societies, to get at essentials, and selects details accordingly. Readers of
Robbe-Grillet who try to imagine a psychology and a motivation for the
characters and to interpret details achieve no deep understanding; at
best they make these texts banal.

Second, Barthes praises Robbe-Grillet for adopting an *écriture* that
'breaks the fascination of narrative'. Novels usually have stories: to read
a novel is to follow a development of some kind. Barthes is surprisingly
uninterested in story. He likes Diderot, Brecht, and Eisenstein, for
example, because each prefers scene to story, dramatic tableau to
narrative development. Barthes likes fragments and devises ways of
fragmenting works with narrative continuity. In Robbe-Grillet's novels,
however, Barthes found texts that resist narrative ordering. It is often
very difficult to piece together a story, to decide, for example, what
'actually happens' and what is memory, hallucination, or narrator's
interpolation. A reader struggling to compose a story is made aware of
the exigencies of narrative ordering, but if one does actually compose a
narrative, one denies the challenge to narrative and misses the point.

These two strategies, of eliminating depth and disrupting narrative, are
what especially interest Barthes; and his early articles 'Objective
Literature' and 'Literal Literature' did much to promote the notion of a
chosiste Robbe-Grillet, devoted above all to objective, dehumanized
descriptions of things that are simply *there*. But as Robbe-Grillet's novels
grew more familiar, it became evident that readers could recuperate
them as literature and make sense of them, particularly by imagining a

narrator. The most mechanical descriptions, the most confusing repetitions or lacunae, make sense if they are taken as the thoughts of a disturbed narrator. *La Jalousie*, with its repeated geometrical descriptions, can be read as the perceptions of a paranoid and obsessed narrator. *Dans le labyrinthe* can be read as the discourse of a narrator suffering from amnesia. Instead of 'objective literature' we have then a literature of subjectivity, taking place entirely within the mind of a deranged narrator.

When asked to write a preface to a book about Robbe-Grillet which did exactly what Barthes's articles had said should not be done, reconstructing plots, positing narrators, identifying symbolic patterns, and providing thematic interpretations, Barthes took a new position. There are two Robbe-Grillets, he argued in 'Le Point sur Robbe-Grillet?': on the one hand, the objectivist; on the other, the humanist or subjectivist. He can be read either way, 'and finally it is this ambiguity which counts, which concerns us, which bears the historical meaning of an oeuvre that seems peremptorily to reject history. What is this meaning? The very opposite of a meaning, i.e., *a question*. What do things signify? What does the world signify?' (*Essais critiques*, p. 203/202). 'Robbe-Grillet's oeuvre becomes the ordeal of meaning experienced by a certain society,' as illustrated in that society's changing engagement with it.

The task of literature, Barthes writes in the preface to *Essais critiques*, is not, as is often thought, *to express the unexpressible* – this would be a 'literature of the soul' as he disdainfully calls it. Literature should attempt, rather, 'to *unexpress the expressible*', to problematize the meanings we automatically confer or assume. Robbe-Grillet is therefore exemplary for Barthes, and the essays collected in *Sollers écrivain* later cast Philippe Sollers, another creator of avant-garde prose, in the same role of attempting to *unwrite* the world as it is written or written out in prior discourse. The writer struggles 'to detach a secondary language from the slime of primary languages afforded him by the world' (*Essais critiques*, p. 15/xvii). This language – perhaps ordered, perhaps elegant – Barthes imagines light and clean, not weighed down or filled with meaning.

This ethics of language, so central to Barthes's promotion of the avant-garde, may help to account for a puzzling feature of his criticism. Despite his broad literary tastes – he likes modern authors and old-fashioned authors, terse authors, and exuberant authors – he takes no interest in poetry. With the exception of Racine, he never writes about verse, and Racine's verse scarcely detains him. No comprehensive theory of poetry explains his neglect, but various passing comments, and the chapter 'Is There a Poetic *Écriture*?' in *Le Degré zéro*, may shed some light on this curious silence.

Several remarks suggest that Barthes associates poetry with symbols, with plenitude of meaning, with attempts to create motivated rather than arbitrary signs, and thus sees it as the aspect of literariness that such heroes as Brecht, Robbe-Grillet, and Sollers are trying to combat. However, in *Le Degré zéro* he takes a different line, arguing that there is no *écriture poétique* because, on the one hand, classical poetry is not based on a distinctive use of language (it is part of the comprehensive *écriture classique*) and, on the other hand, modern poetry is 'a language in which a violent drive towards autonomy destroys any ethical scope'. One might expect him to take a lively interest in what he calls this 'discourse full of gaps and flashes, full of absences and voracious signs, without fixed and stable intentions', but he goes on to write of modern poetry's attempt to destroy language and reduce discourse to 'words as static things' (pp. 38–9/48–51). And in *Mythologies* he claims that poetry attempts to achieve a pre-semiological state in which it would present the thing itself.

Since Barthes shows no inclination to believe that poetry does present an unmediated reality, and since the questionable ambitions he attributes to it seem to resemble those of a *chosiste* Robbe-Grillet, one is

Critic

led to suppose that there is something else at stake, that other forces in Barthes's critical practice work to produce this neglect of poetry. Though *Le Degré zéro* set poetry aside by denying that there was an *écriture poétique*, one can contend that there is in fact an *écriture poétique*, whose connotations of richness, density, and depth of meaning are so powerful as to frustrate the most resolutely anti-poetic poetry. When read as poetry, a sentence such as 'Yesterday I went into town and bought a lamp' draws upon symbolic codes (illumination, commerce) and conventional presumptions of meaning to create rich possibilities of signification. (If the poem consists solely of this minimal sentence, one can find meaning in the absence of any further statement.) In *L'Empire des signes* Barthes writes that for the Westerner haiku is a seductive form because you record a single impression and 'your sentence, whatever it may be, will articulate a lesson, release a symbol, you will be profound, effortlessly, your writing will be *full*' (p. 92/70). Our Western *écriture poétique* creates a presumption of symbolic plenitude and leads us to read haiku accordingly (whereas Barthes imagines that in his utopian Japan they remain empty). For the Westerner, it is difficult to escape fullness of signification in poetry, while in long prose forms the pressure of symbolic meaning is less intense. By excluding poetry from his criticism, Barthes attempts to free literature from the richness of meaning associated with it.

Barthes also makes poetry a scapegoat in a different way. At the end of *Mythologies* he remarks, 'by poetry I understand, in a very general way, the search for the inalienable meaning of things' (p. 247/151). He allows poetry mythically to represent for him the quest for a pre-semiological Nature or Truth, so that this project can be cast out of the domain of literature by setting poetry aside. In *What is Literature?* Sartre had distinguished between poetry (playing with language) and prose (using language to discuss the world) so as to exclude linguistic play from consideration by ignoring poetry. The terms of Barthes's distinction are quite different – for him it is *prose* that experiments with language while poetry attempts to transcend or destroy it – but structurally he is

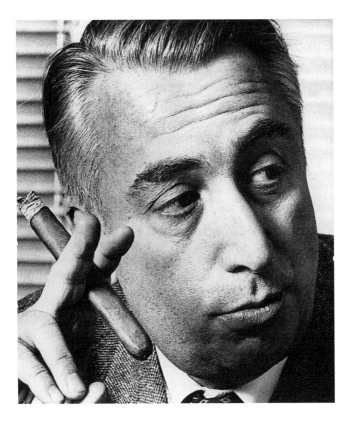

6. Barthes with cigar.

engaged in the same operation: by dubiously identifying some important general aspect of literature with the poetic, he can ignore this quality or project by declining to discuss poetry.

One factor remains. In his inaugural lecture at the Collège de France, Barthes declared, 'By *literature* I understand not a body or a sequence of works, nor even a commercial domain or area of instruction, but the complex inscription of the traces of a practice: the practice of writing' (*Leçon*, p. 16/462). Interested in writing practices rather than achieved forms, he is inclined to neglect sonnets, for example, in favour of interminable prose writings that he can cut to his own liking, creating powerful fragments that can be mobilized in his critical discourse. He does not elucidate tightly constructed forms but celebrates a semiotic activity, which is doubtless why so many of his writings about literature take unorthodox forms.

Chapter 5
Polemicist

In 1963 Barthes published essays on contemporary criticism in the *Times Literary Supplement* and the American journal *Modern Language Notes* informing his readers that there were two sorts of criticism in France, a dreary and positivistic academic criticism (*la critique universitaire*) and a lively, variegated, interpretative criticism (soon baptized '*la nouvelle critique*'), whose practitioners sought not to establish facts about a work but to explore its meaning from a modern theoretical or philosophical standpoint. When these polemical pieces were reprinted in *Essais critiques* the following year, the academy was annoyed. The review in *Le Monde* (16 March 1964) by Raymond Picard, professor at the Sorbonne, ignored the rest of the volume to concentrate on this 'futile and irresponsible defamation', which might give an uninformed foreign audience the wrong idea of the French university.

But it may not have been altogether the wrong idea. To advance as a teacher in the French university system, one had to be making visible progress on a *Doctorat d'État*, a massive scholarly thesis seldom completed in less than ten years, whose goal was solidly documented knowledge. This is not a genre that encourages methodological innovation, theoretical speculation, or unorthodox interpretation, and the critics who have done most to enliven and advance literary studies in France for the most part worked outside the university system, supporting themselves by their writing (Jean-Paul Sartre, Maurice

Blanchot), by teaching abroad (Georges Poulet, René Girard, Louis Marin, Jean-Pierre Richard), or working in special institutions which may use other criteria in their appointments (Barthes, Gérard Genette, Tzvetan Todorov, Lucien Goldmann). After 1968 the situation in universities changed somewhat, but in the early 1960s Barthes's distinction was not altogether inaccurate.

Barthes makes two complaints against academic criticism. While interpretative critics make clear their philosophical or ideological allegiances – to existentialism, Marxism, phenomenology, psychoanalysis, semiotics – academic criticism claims objectivity, pretends to have no ideology. Without theoretical argument, it claims to know the essential nature of literature, and it eclectically accepts or rejects, in the name of common sense, everything offered by ideologically committed criticism. It will reject Freudian or Marxist interpretations as exaggerated or far-fetched (instinctively, Barthes says, it applies the brakes), without granting that this rejection implies an alternative psychology or theory of society that ought to be formulated. The mild-mannered eclecticism of traditional criticism is in fact the most presumptuous ideology of all, since it claims to know under what circumstances every other method might be right and when it is wrong. The concealment of ideology as common sense is what Barthes objects to most strongly.

Second, and this argument will be less familiar to English and American readers, Barthes claims that what academic criticism rejects is immanent interpretation. It wants to explain the work in terms of facts outside the work about the author's world or his sources. Since it sees the literary work as a reproduction of something outside it, it will, under certain conditions, accept psychoanalytic readings as valid but partial views, if they explain the work in terms of the author's past, or admit Marxist readings, if they explain it in terms of historical realities. What it will not accept, Barthes argues, is 'that interpretation and ideology can decide to work in a domain entirely within the work'. Barthes argues that the use of theoretical languages to explore the structure of a work is quite different from approaches that seek causal explanations outside the work. An immanent reading using psychoanalytical concepts to elucidate the dynamics of a work has little in common with the psychoanalytical attempt to explain the work as the product of an author's psyche. Academic criticism in France, says Barthes, is hostile to immanent analysis because it associates knowledge with causal explanation and because it is easier to evaluate students' knowledge than their interpretations. A theory of literature predicated on the importance of knowledge about the author's life and times lends itself to examinations and grading.

Picard may have been equally annoyed by an essay he does not mention, 'Histoire ou littérature' in *Sur Racine*, which astutely discusses the failings of a number of critical books on Racine, including Picard's own doctoral theis, *La Carrière de Jean Racine* – one of many 'admirable' works serving 'a confused cause' (p. 167/172). Professors committed to literary history, Barthes argues, have allowed their fascination with the author and his doings to eclipse the questions that genuinely require historical answers: questions about the history of the literary function or literary institution in Racine's age. For Picard, 'history is still, fatally, the raw material for a portrait.' 'If one wants to write literary history, one must renounce the individual Racine and deliberately move to the level of techniques, rules, rites and collective mentalities', discussing the general pattern of literary careers in the period (pp. 154, 167/159, 172). When critics do concentrate on Racine as the source of his tragedies, which is interpretation rather than history, their inclination is always 'to apply the brakes', as though 'the timidity and banality of the hypothesis were proof of its validity' (p. 160/166). In connecting author and works, they must rely on a psychology, and they are most timid precisely when they should boldly declare the psychology on which they rely.

Of all the approaches to man, psychology is the most unprovable [*improbable*], the most marked by its time. This is because, in fact, *knowledge* of the profound self is illusory: there are only different ways of articulating it. Racine lends himself to several languages – psychoanalytic, existential, tragic, psychological (others can be invented, others will be invented); none is innocent. But to acknowledge this incapacity to *tell the truth* about Racine is precisely to acknowledge, at last, the special status of literature.

p. 166/171

This was what Picard could not accept, as he made clear in the little book *Nouvelle critique ou nouvelle imposture?*, with which he returned to the fray the following year: 'There is a truth about Racine', he declared, 'on which everyone can manage to agree. By relying, in particular, on the certainties of language; the implications of psychological coherence, and the structural requirements of the genre, the patient and modest researcher does succeed in bringing out indisputable facts that in some measure determine zones of objectivity (it is from these that he can – very cautiously – hazard interpretations).'[9] Attacking the interpretative critics Barthes's articles had praised, but especially Barthes's *Sur Racine*, Picard sought to combat the 'dangers' *la nouvelle critique* posed to literary study and to the principles of clarity, coherence, and logic. He develops four charges: (1) that, combining impressionism and ideological dogmatism, Barthes makes irresponsible, unsupportable statements about Racine's plays; (2) that his theory leads to a relativism in which the critic can say anything at all (*n'importe quoi*), since it asks only that the critic admit the subjectivity of his view; (3) that Barthes has the execrable taste to import into the plays an 'obsessive, unbridled and cynical sexuality', such that 'one must reread Racine to persuade oneself that his characters are different from those of D. H. Lawrence'; and (4) that Barthes develops a mystificatory, pseudo-scientific jargon to imply a rigour that is altogether lacking.

Although Picard is convincing in his demonstration that many of

Barthes

Barthes's claims about Racinean man hold for only a few of the characters in question, what attracted attention and created a great literary quarrel was Picard's spirited defence of the cultural patrimony against irreverent ideologies and their jargon. As far as one could judge from the outpouring of congratulatory articles that greeted *Nouvelle critique ou nouvelle imposture?*, at stake were two deep principles manifested in confused but firmly held beliefs: that the glory of the national cultural heritage depended upon the determinacy of meaning and the truth of the past (the Racine one had studied should not change meaning), and that to contest the artist's conscious control or to ignore intended meaning was to offer a general challenge to subjects' ability to grasp themselves and their world. One writer in *Le Monde* explicitly set forth what Barthes had previously satirized in *Mythologies* as the bourgeois attitude toward criticism (that its task was to declare that Racine is Racine). True criticism, wrote this contributor to the debate, seeks to understand the past for its own sake and 'refuses to revise it. . . . It looks for *Racine* in Racine and not the metamorphoses Racine undergoes in coming into contact with ideologies or jargons.'[10] In 'Racine is Racine' Barthes had observed that while this tautology is illusory, since there are only versions of Racine,

> we understand, at least, what such vacuity in definition affords those who brandish it so proudly: a kind of minor ethical salvation, the satisfaction of having militated for a truth of Racine without having to assume the risks which any actual search inevitably involves. Tautology dispenses us from having ideas, but at the same time prides itself on making this licence into a stern morality; whence its success – laziness promoted to the rank of rigour. Racine is Racine: admirable security of nothingness.
>
> *Mythologies*, p. 98/*The Eiffel Tower*, p. 61

Picard's attack made Barthes the spokesman for *la nouvelle critique*, praised or blamed by all those who volunteered to adjudicate the controversy. In *Critique et vérité* Barthes responded not to Picard's disagreements about Racine but to the general issues that had been raised. His principal argument, of course, is that what Picard cites as foundations (the certainties of language, the implications of psychological coherence, and the structural requirements of the genre) are already interpretations, based on an ideology which academic critics wished to present as reason itself. Barthes claims that the major issue is academic criticism's resistance to the symbolic nature of language, particularly to ambiguity and connotation. Certainly Picard is most vigorously normative when rejecting connotations of various kinds: 'one does not have the *right* to see an evocation of water in the formulation "rentrer dans le port" [come back into harbour], or a precise allusion to the respiratory mechanism in the expression "*respirer à vos pieds*" [to take respite at your feet]' (pp. 66-7/20). Barthes emphasizes that such claims require theoretical substantiation, an argument about literary language and the conventions and purposes of criticism. They cannot be taken for granted, though all the inclinations of *l'ancienne critique* are to appeal to what goes without saying and charge *la nouvelle critique* with going too far.

For Barthes, of course, interpretation should be extravagant. Criticism that remained within received opinion would have no point or savour. Barthes's writing has always fed controversy: its laconic pronouncements irritate those who hold other views. But Barthes seldom takes part in debates he has provoked and in later years he became increasingly 'laxist', as he put it: uncompromising in his own formulations but uninterested in challenging others or in defending his own positions. Buoyed by success, he was able to indulge in what he wryly calls in his inaugural lecture 'a personal inclination to escape an intellectual difficulty by exploring my own pleasure' (*Leçon*, p. 8/458).

In *Critique et vérité*, however, he did, however reluctantly, rise to the occasion of debate to produce in part II his most lucid and convincing programme for literary studies. Suggesting that the task of a nation's criticism might be to 'take up periodically the objects of its past and

7. Distress, boredom.

describe them anew, to discover *what it can make of them*', Barthes distinguishes between *criticism*, which assumes the risk of placing the work in a situation and expounding a meaning, and a *science of literature*, or poetics, which analyses the conditions of meaning, treating the work as an empty form that can be given meaning by the times in which it is read. The critic is a writer attempting to cover the work with his language, to generate a meaning by deriving it from the work. Poetics, on the other hand, does not interpret works but attempts to describe the structures and the conventions of reading that have made them intelligible, enabling them to bear the range of meanings they have borne for readers of different eras and persuasions.

Pressed by Picard, Barthes articulated an eminently logical and defensible position, but he could not live by its central distinction. Given his conviction that literature is a critique of meaning, he does not like to spend his time filling in meaning; yet his interest in trying out languages on works of the past and the present prevents him from restricting himself to investigations of the structures and codes that have made works intelligible. *Critique et vérité* does not give us Barthes's position, but it provides an excellent account of criticism and a lucid programme for a structuralist science of literature, or poetics.

Chapter 6
Semiologist

Semiology, the general science of signs, was proposed by Ferdinand de Saussure, the founder of modern linguistics, in the early years of the 20th century but remained just an idea until the 1960s, when anthropologists, literary critics, and others, impressed by the success of linguistics, sought to profit from its methodological insights and found themselves developing the semiological science that Saussure had postulated.[11] Barthes was an early advocate of semiology and much later, in choosing the title of his chair at the Collège de France, named semiology as his field, though he stressed in his inaugural lecture that his personal semiology was quite tangential, if not inimical, to the growing discipline he had once promoted.

To discuss Barthes as semiologist, then, is both to identify a continuing concern and to focus on the way he values new approaches for their explanatory energy and power of estrangement but rebels as soon as the possibility of orthodoxy arises. The source of his original attraction seems clear. In *Mythologies* he discovered that various linguistic terms could give him a new perspective on cultural phenomena, and he enthusiastically embraced the possibility of studying all human activity as a series of 'languages'. 'It seemed to me that a science of signs could stimulate social criticism and that Sartre, Brecht, and Saussure could join forces in this project' (*Leçon*, p. 32/471). Part of the attraction was the hope that a formal discipline which required one to name signifiers and signifieds would display convincingly the ideological contents of various activities. But the point of a new discipline or new vocabulary was above all to force one to look closely at what goes without saying and to make explicit what one implicitly knows: in order to apply the new terms or perform the new operations one must rethink familiar practices.

New approaches have a *Verfremdungseffekt*, a power of estrangement, that can be lost as the discipline itself becomes an orthodoxy. Barthes could continue to think of himself as a semiologist, it seems, only by defining semiology as a perspective that questions other established disciplines. In *Leçon* he jokes that he hopes to make his Chair of Literary Semiology into a wheelchair, always on the move, 'the wildcard [*joker*] of contemporary knowledge' (p. 38/474). He describes his semiology as the 'undoing' of linguistics, or, more specifically, as the study of all aspects of signification set aside as impure by a scientific linguistics. It is 'the labour that collects the impurity of language, the waste of linguistics, the immediate corruption of any message: nothing less than the desires, fears, expressions, intimidations, advances, blandishments, protests, excuses, aggressions and melodies of which active language is made' (pp. 31–2/470–1). Throughout his career Barthes retains the notion of semiology as a bringing into the open of aspects of meaning ignored by orthodox disciplines. As semiotics becomes an established field, Barthes's semiology changes from a promotion of a science of signs to an activity on its margins.

He did make a brief stab at establishing an orthodoxy himself in *Éléments de sémiologie* (1964), which set forth the basic concepts of a fledgling discipline – the distinctions between *langue* and *parole, signifier* and *signified*, and *syntagmatic* and *paradigmatic* relations – and speculated how they might apply to various non-linguistic phenomena. Semiology, he says, must first of all 'try itself out'; playing public experimenter, Barthes tries out linguistic concepts he thinks may prove useful in studying other signifying phenomena.

Most important is Saussure's distinction between *langue* and *parole*. *La langue* is the linguistic system, what one learns when one learns a language, and *parole* is speech, the innumerable utterances, spoken and written, of a language. Linguistics, and by analogy semiology, attempts to describe the underlying system of rules and distinctions that makes possible signifying events. Semiology is based on the premise that insofar as human actions and objects have meaning, there must be a system of distinctions and conventions, conscious or unconscious, that generates that meaning. For a semiologist studying the food system of a culture, for example, *parole* consists of all the events of eating and *langue* is the system of rules underlying these events, rules that define what is edible, what dishes go with or contrast with one another, how they are combined to form meals; in short, all the rules and prescriptions that enable meals to be culturally orthodox or unorthodox. A restaurant menu represents a sample of a society's 'food grammar'. There are 'syntactic' slots (soups, appetizers; entrées, salads, desserts) and paradigm classes of contrasting items that can fill each slot (the soups among which one chooses). There are conventions governing the syntactic ordering of items within a meal (*soup, main course, dessert* is orthodox, while *dessert, main course, soup* is ungrammatical). And the contrasts between dishes within classes, such as *main course* or *dessert*, bear meaning: hamburger and roast pheasant have different second-order meanings. Approaching such material with the linguistic model, the semiologist has a clear task: to reconstruct the system of distinctions and conventions that enable a group of phenomena to have the meaning they do for members of a culture.

A striking feature of Barthes's account is his claim that language is not just the prime example of a semiological system but also the reality on which the semiologist always relies; in effect never studying anything but language. He goes so far as to claim that Saussure was wrong to make linguistics a branch of semiology, and that semiology is really a branch of a comprehensive linguistics: it is the study of how language

8. At the Collège de France, 7 January 1978: Barthes's inaugural lecture.

articulates the world. When semiologists investigate the food system or clothing system of a particular culture and try to discover its signifying units and contrasts, they get their best clues from the language in which clothes or food are discussed, from what this language names and does not name. 'Who can be sure', Barthes asks, 'that in passing from whole-wheat bread to white bread, or from toque to bonnet, we pass from one signified to another? In most cases, the semiologist will have some institutional mediators, or metalanguages, which will supply him with the signifieds he needs for his commutations: the article on gastronomy or the fashion magazine' (*Éléments de sémiologie*, pp. 139–40/66).

Even if language were the only evidence semiologists had, this would not make semiology part of linguistics any more than historians' reliance on written documents makes history a part of linguistics. But semiologists cannot rely on language alone; they cannot assume that everything named is significant and everything unnamed insignificant, especially when studying what-goes-without-saying. For Barthes, however, the evidence of language proved methodologically indispensable in his one large-scale semiological study, *Système de la mode*. Fashion is a system that creates meaning by differentiating garments, endowing details with significance, and establishing links between certain aspects of clothing and worldly activities. '*C'est le sens qui fait vendre*', Barthes writes; it's meaning that sells (p. 10/xii). To describe this system Barthes takes the captions beneath photographs in a year's issues of two fashion magazines, on the assumption that the captions will call attention to the aspects of the garment that make it fashionable and thus enable him to identify the distinctions at work in this sign system.

Barthes discovers three levels of signification, nicely illustrated by a couple of examples: *Les imprimés triomphent aux courses* (Prints win at the races) and *Une petite ganse fait l'élégance* (Slim piping is striking). At the level of what Barthes calls the 'vestimentary code', the code of what is fashionable, *prints* and *piping* are signifiers whose signified is *fashionable*. At a second level, the joining together of prints and races suggests the appropriateness of these dresses in a certain social milieu. Finally, there is 'a new type of sign whose signifier is the fashion utterance in its complete form and whose signified is the image of the world and of fashion that the journal has or wants to convey' (p. 47/36). These captions imply, for example, that piping is not just considered elegant but actually produces elegance (*fait l'élégance)* and that prints are the crucial and active agents of social triumphs (life is a competition which your clothes win or lose for you). Barthes calls the second and third levels the 'rhetorical system' of fashion.

The vestimentary code is important but not especially interesting to read about; Barthes works diligently with a large corpus of fashion captions, analysing the variations on which fashion seems to rely. He encounters some methodological difficulties: in particular, a truly

61

perspicuous analysis would require information about what combinations are impossible or unfashionable.[12] Far more interesting, for both Barthes and his readers, is the rhetorical system, the mythical level of fashion. Fashion obeys the law of myth in its attempt to present its conventions as natural facts. *This summer dresses will be of silk*, the caption tells us, as if announcing an inevitable natural occurrence; *Dresses are becoming longer*, inexorably. The captions announce how useful these garments will be – *Just the thing for cool summer evenings* – but the specificity of some uses is puzzling. Why, for example, *A raincoat for evening strolls along the docks at Calais*? Barthes notes that:

> It is the very preciseness of the reference to the world that makes the function unreal; once again we encounter the paradox of the art of the novel: any function so minutely detailed becomes unreal, but at the same time, the more contingent the function, the more 'natural' it seems. Fashion writing thus comes back to the postulate of realist style, according to which an accumulation of minute and precise details accredits the truth of the thing represented.
>
> p. 268/266

Fashion energetically and resourcefully naturalizes its signs because it must make what it can of small differences, proclaiming the importance of trivial modifications. *Cette année les étoffes velues succèdent aux étoffes poilues* (This year fuzzy fabrics replace shaggy ones). The distinction is what matters, not its content. Fashion 'is the spectacle to which human beings treat themselves of the power they have to make the insignificant signify' (p. 287/288). Or, as Barthes puts it in *Essais critiques*, 'fashion and literature signify strongly, subtly, with all the complexities of an extreme art, but, if you will, they signify "nothing", their being is in the signifying, not in what is signified' (p. 156/152).

Barthes's most systematic semiological study leads to conclusions that are increasingly emphasized in later writings which, paradoxically, reject the idea of a 'science' of signs. 'I passed through a euphoric dream of scientificity', he says dismissively of the early 1960s ('Réponses', p. 97). Defining semiology as attention to everything that makes a science of signification impossible, he associates his rejection of science with the priority of signifying over what is signified, choosing to ignore that this persistent view of meaning emerged from and is substantiated by the systematic perspective he now denigrates. Only by showing fashion or literature to be a system, a mechanism that endlessly elaborates meaning, can Barthes maintain the priority of signifying over what is signified. Taken individually, outside the perspective of a system, fashion statements have meanings that seem more important than any process of signification. Only by convincingly identifying the systematic functioning of a semiological mechanism can one demonstrate the irrelevance of the content of particular fashion captions and give weight to the notion of fashion or literature as systems that undermine or empty the meanings they luxuriantly produce.

Moreover, though Barthes later wished to present his semiology as an attention to all aspects of meaning that resist scientific analysis, what he notices about meaning in his later works is interesting precisely because it suggests general claims about further levels of signification. When he notes that his remark to the woman at the bakery about the beauty of the light bears the marks of a class sensibility, this is certainly not science, but it is interesting and perceptive because it suggests how far an investigation of signs of class membership would have to extend. When he comments that the conventions of academic discussion

9. The history of semiology.

require one to respond to the ostensible content of a question rather than to the underlying attitude it expresses, he is identifying a subject for investigation: the relation between the specific content and the primary force of speech acts and how different conventions direct responses towards one or the other. Secure in his 'wheelchair', Barthes no longer needed to accompany his insights with the call for a science to extend and exploit them; he could speak of his desire to produce a discourse without power, which would not seek to impose itself but rather be a pleasant excursion (*Leçon*, p. 42/476). The interest of his discourse would continue to lie, however, in the potentially systematic reflections on signs and meaning that it provoked. For where there is meaning, there is system. It is Barthes who taught us that.

Chapter 7
Structuralist

The ready answer to the question 'Who is Roland Barthes?' is 'a French structuralist'. Although Barthes's greatest admirers might insist that structuralism was only a moment in his varied career, and not the moment in which he was most truly himself, it is the most important moment: the source of his influence, the fruition of projects and attitudes, and the springboard for future manoeuvres. When structuralism had become a source of authority, Barthes could comfortably take his distance from it, allowing others to see him as a 'post-structuralist', but this produced considerable confusion, for to invent 'post-structuralism' one had to reduce structuralism to a narrow caricature. Much of what was heralded as 'post-structuralist' was in fact already conspicuous in structuralist writings.

In an article of 1967 for the *Times Literary Supplement* Barthes defined structuralism as a way of analysing cultural artefacts that originates in the methods of linguistics (*Le Bruissement de la langue*, p. 13/5). And in *Essais critiques* he explains that he has 'been engaged in a series of structural analyses all of which aim at defining a number of non-linguistic languages' (p. 155/151–2). Treating phenomena as the products of underlying systems of rules and distinctions, structuralism takes from linguistics two cardinal principles: that signifying entities do not have essences but are defined by networks of relations, both internal and external, and that to account for signifying phenomena is to describe the system of norms that makes them possible. Structural explanation does not seek historical antecedents or causes but discusses the structure and significance of particular objects or actions by relating them to the system within which they function.

In the 1960s there seemed no reason to try to distinguish structuralism and semiology. Defining 'the structuralist activity' in *Essais critiques*, Barthes declared that 'serious recourse to the nomenclature of signification' was the mark of structuralism and advised interested readers to 'watch who uses *signifier* and *signified, synchrony* and *diachrony*' (pp. 213–14/214). Eventually, though, semiology (or semiotics) came to be seen as a field of study – the study of sign systems of all sorts – while 'structuralism' came to denote the claims and procedures of French writings of the 1960s that sought to describe the underlying structures of a range of human activities. 'The goal of all structuralist activity,' Barthes wrote, 'whether reflexive or poetic, is to "reconstitute" an object so as to manifest the rules of its functioning.' 'What is new', he concluded, 'is a mode of thought (or a "poetics") which seeks less to assign completed meanings to the objects it discovers than to know how meaning is possible, at what cost and by what means' (p. 218/218). He urges the student of literature

> to take as a moral goal not the decipherment of a work's meaning but the reconstruction of the rules and constraints of that meaning's elaboration. . . . The critic is not responsible for reconstructing the work's message but only its system, just as the linguist is not responsible for deciphering the sentence's meaning but for establishing the formal structure that permits this meaning to be transmitted.
>
> pp. 259–60/256–7

In order to understand the functioning of the most interesting and innovatory literary works, one must reconstruct the systems of norms they parody, resist, or disrupt.

One can distinguish four aspects of the structuralist study of literature. First, there is the attempt to describe the language of literature in linguistic terms so as to capture the distinctiveness of literary structures. Barthes frequently employs linguistic categories in discussing literary discourse; he is particularly interested in Émile Benveniste's distinction between linguistic forms that contain some reference to the situation of enunciation (first and second person pronouns, expressions such as *here, there, yesterday*, and certain verb tenses) and forms that do not. This distinction helps Barthes to analyse some aspects of narrative technique, but he has a piratical approach to linguistics and does not attempt systematic linguistic descriptions as some structuralists do.[13]

The second major project is the development of a 'narratology' that identifies the constituents of narrative and their possible combinations in different narrative techniques. Building on the work of the Russian formalist Vladimir Propp, whose 'grammar' of folktales describes basic motifs and their possibilities of combination, French structuralists

10. Barthes at his desk.

concentrated particularly on plot, asking what its basic elements are, how they combine, what the elementary plot structures are, and how effects of completeness and incompleteness are produced. Barthes wrote a long introduction to a special issue of *Communications* on this subject ('Introduction to the Structural Analysis of Narratives' in *Image, Music, Text*), and his later works emphasize both the role of plot structures in assuring the intelligibility of writing and the effects that can be produced by disrupting narrative expectations. It is impossible to produce a narrative 'without reference to an implicit system of units and rules', he writes (*Image, Music, Text*, p. 81); it is only in relation to conventional narrative expectations that constructions can be excessive or deceptive.

In addition to the systematic study of narrative, structuralists attempt to show how literary meaning depends upon the codes produced by prior discourses of a culture. The most important contribution to this project is Barthes's *S/Z*, which I shall discuss in a moment. Finally, structuralism promotes analysis of the reader's role in producing meaning and of the ways literary works achieve their effects by resisting or complying with readers' expectations. Introduced by Barthes's discussions of Robbe-Grillet, this concern takes two different forms in his later writings. First, there is a claim that words and thus works have meaning only in relation to discursive conventions and habits of reading, which must be studied if one is to understand literary structure. The reader thus becomes important as the repository of conventions, the agent of their application. Poetics focuses on the intelligibility of the work and brings in the reader not as a person or a subjectivity but as a role: the embodiment of the codes that permit reading. 'The "I" that approaches the text', Barthes writes, 'is itself already a plurality of other texts, of codes which are infinite or, more precisely, lost (whose origin is lost). . . . Subjectivity is generally imagined as a plenitude with which I encumber the text, but in fact this faked plenitude is only the wake of all the codes that constitute me, so that ultimately my subjectivity has the generality of stereotypes' (*S/Z*, pp. 16–17/10). This reader also appears in a second claim: that the most interesting or most valuable literature is that which most vigorously exercises the reader, challenging and calling attention to the structuring activity of reading. 'What is at stake in literary work (in literature as work) is making the reader no longer a consumer but a producer of the text' (p. 10/4). Structuralism has presided over the emergence of the reader as a central figure in criticism, and if, as Barthes says, 'the birth of the reader must be requited by the death of the Author,' who is no longer treated as the source and arbiter of meaning, this is a price he is willing to pay (*Le Bruissement de la langue*, p. 69/55).

The structuralist attempt to understand how we make sense of a text leads one to think of literature not as a representation or communication but as a series of forms produced by the institution of literature and the discursive codes of a culture. Structural analysis does not move towards the discovery of secret meanings: a work is like an onion, Barthes writes, 'a construction of layers (or levels, or systems), whose body contains, finally, no heart, no kernel, no secret, no irreducible principle, nothing except the infinity of its own envelopes – which envelop nothing other than the unity of its own surfaces' (*Le Bruissement de la langue*, p. 159/99). A structural analysis does not produce an 'explanation' of a text but begins with an initial view of its content and enters into the play of the codes that are responsible, 'identifying their terms, sketching their sequences, but also postulating other codes, which will appear in the perspective of the first ones.'[4] As he puts it in 'La Mort de l'auteur',

> In the multiplicity of writing, everything is to be *disentangled*, nothing *deciphered*; the structure can be followed, 'run' (like the thread of a stocking) at every point and at every level, but there is nothing beneath: the space of writing is to be ranged over, not pierced; writing ceaselessly posits meaning ceaselessly to evaporate it, carrying out a systematic exemption of meaning. In precisely this way literature (it would be better

from now on to say *writing*), by refusing to assign a 'secret', an ultimate meaning, to the text (and to the world-as-text), liberates an activity we may call counter-theological, an activity that is truly revolutionary since to refuse to fix meaning is, in the end, to refuse God and his hypostases – reason, science, law.

Le Bruissement de la langue, p. 68/53–4

A disentangling which 'runs' threads of meaning: this is the mode of Barthes's most ambitious and sustained structural analysis, *S/Z*, a line-by-line discussion of Balzac's novella *Sarrasine*. Breaking the text into fragments, or 'lexias', as he calls them, he identifies the codes on which they rely. Each code is the accumulated cultural knowledge that enables a reader to recognize details as contributions to a particular function or sequence The *proairetic code*, for example (Barthes often draws upon Greek to create technical terms), is a series of models of action that help readers place details in plot sequences: because we have stereotyped models of 'falling in love', or 'kidnapping', or 'undertaking a perilous mission', we can tentatively place and organize the details we encounter as we read. The *hermeneutic code* governs mystery and suspense, helping us to recognize what counts as an enigma and arrange details as possible contributions to its solution. The *semic code* provides cultural stereotypes (models of personality, for example) that enable readers to gather pieces of information to create characters; and the *symbolic code* guides the extrapolation from textual details to symbolic interpretations. What Barthes calls the *referential code* in *S/Z* is later divided into a series of cultural codes that are most easily thought of as so many manuals providing the cultural information on which texts rely.[15] When Balzac writes that Count Lanty was 'as gloomy as a Spaniard and as boring as a banker', he draws upon cultural stereotypes. When he writes that coming out of the theatre where he has seen Zambinella sing, Sarrasine is 'overcome with an inexplicable sadness', our models of cultural verisimilitude let us read this as a mark of deep involvement. 'Although entirely derived from books, these codes, by a reversal characteristic to bourgeois ideology, which turns culture into nature, serve as the foundation of the real, of "Life" ' (*S/Z*, p. 211/206).

In identifying codes and commenting on their functioning in classic and modernist literature, Barthes seeks not to interpret *Sarrasine* but to analyse it as an intertextual construct, the product of various cultural discourses. 'We now know', he writes in 'La Mort de l'auteur', 'that the text is not a line of words releasing a single "theological" meaning (the "message" of an Author-God) but a multi-dimensional space in which a variety of writings, none of them original, blend and clash. The text is a tissue of quotations drawn from innumerable sources of culture' (*Le Bruissement de la langue*, p.67/52–3). Attentive to this citational play of codes, he describes, for example, the ironic strategies of readable literature. Referential codes can easily become boring in their conformism:

> The classic remedy . . . is to treat them ironically by superimposing a second code that enunciates them with detachment . . . In saying that Sarrasine 'had hoped for a dimly lit room, a jealous rival, death and love, etc.', the discourse mingles three staggered codes . . . The Code of Passion establishes what Sarrasine is supposed to be feeling; the Novelistic Code transforms this 'feeling' into literature: it is the code of an innocent author who has no doubt that the novelistic is a *just* (natural) expression of passion. The Ironic Code takes up the 'naïveté' of the first two codes: as the novelist undertakes to speak of the character (code 2), the ironist undertakes to speak of the novelist (code 3) . . . it would suffice to produce . . . a pastiche of Balzac to take one step further this staggering of codes. The effect of this cantilevering? Constantly going beyond the previous stage and aspiring to infinity, it constitutes writing in all the power of its play.
>
> *S/Z*, p. 145/139

Readable writing allows the reader to determine which is the final code (say, the implication, 'this is ironic'). An author like Flaubert, however,

11. Seminar at the École pratique des hautes études, 1974.

in wielding an irony fraught with uncertainty, brings about a salutary uneasiness in writing: he refuses to halt the play of codes (or does so badly), with the result that (and this is no doubt the true test of writing) one never knows whether he is responsible for what he writes (whether there is a subject behind his language): for the essence of writing (the meaning of the work which constitutes it) is to prevent any reply to the question: who is speaking?

p. 146/140

Barthes's breaking up of the text in pursuit of codes enables him to do close reading while resisting the presumption of Anglo-American close reading that every detail must be shown to contribute to the aesthetic unity of the whole. Interested in the 'plural' qualities of the work, he refuses to seek an overall unifying structure but asks how each detail works, what codes it relates to, and proves adept at discovering functions.[16] Apparently gratuitous descriptive details, for instance, by their 'failure to relate to any of the codes advancing the plot, revealing character, contributing to suspense, or generating symbolic meaning, produce a 'reality effect': by their very resistance to meaning they signify, 'this is the real.'[17]

The paradox of *S/Z* is that its categories explicitly denigrate classic, readable literature, of which Balzac is the epitome, and yet its analysis endows a Balzacian novella with an intriguing and powerful complexity. *S/Z* is predicated upon a distinction between the readable and the writerly, between classic writing that complies with our expectations and avant-garde writing that we don't know how to read but must in effect compose in our reading. Declaring that 'the writerly is our value,' *S/Z* nonetheless takes up a readerly story, but instead of revealing a boring predictability, the analysis opens the story up, presenting it as an astute and resourceful reflection upon its own codes and the signifying mechanisms of its culture. '*Sarrasine* represents the very confusion of representation, the unbridled (pandemic) circulation of signs, sexes and fortunes' (p. 222/216). By declaring the superiority of disruptive, avant-garde literature, *S/Z* helps to produce an intellectual climate in which lovers of Balzac can try to rescue his novels from an appreciative classical reading and treat his works as writing that explores its own signifying procedures. And Barthes's analysis here is exemplary in its effect: in general, structural analyses predicated upon a distinction between works that comply with conventions and works that violate them end up discovering a radical literary practice in the most unexpected, most traditional places – thus subverting the notion of literary *history* as well as Barthes's initial distinction. This is one of the major accomplishments (and perhaps the secret goal) of Barthes's structuralism.

S/Z is Barthes's *summa* – a compendium of his views on literature and a meeting ground for projects often held to be contradictory. On the one hand, it displays a powerful scientific and metalinguistic drive, breaking the work into its constituents, naming and classifying in a rationalist and scientific spirit. In its attempt to explain how readers make sense of novels, it contributes to the poetics outlined in *Critique et vérité*. Yet *S/Z* opens with what Barthes and others have regarded as a renunciation of the structuralist project: Barthes insists that instead of treating the work as the manifestation of an underlying system he will explore its difference from itself, its unmasterable evasiveness, and the way it outplays the codes on which it seems to be based (p. 9/3). The fact that *S/Z* has been seen as an extreme example of both structuralism and post-structuralism suggests that we ought to regard this distinction with suspicion. From the very beginning, we should remember, structuralist attempts to describe the codes of literary discourse were linked with an exploration of how avant-garde works, such as Robbe-Grillet's, foreground, parody, and violate those conventions.

There is, of course, a contrast between the scientific ambitions of structuralism and, for example, the version of post-structuralism called 'deconstruction',[18] which characteristically shows how discourses undermine the philosophical presuppositions on which they rely; but one may easily make too much of this difference. Structuralist writings repeatedly appeal to linguistic models in order to shift the focus of critical thinking from subjects to discourse, from authors as sources of meaning to systems of convention operating within the discursive systems of a social practice. Meaning is seen as the effect of codes and conventions – sometimes of violating conventions. To describe these conventions, structuralism posits various sciences – a general science of signs, a science of mythology, a science of literature – which serve as the methodological horizon for a range of analytical projects. But within each project attention characteristically focuses on marginal or problematical phenomena which help to identify the conventions that exclude them and whose force depends on these conventions. The notion of a science or complete 'grammar' of forms serves as the methodological horizon for work that focuses in practice on the ungrammatical or the deviant, as in anthropological studies of pollution or taboo or in Michel Foucault's structuralist studies of madness and of incarceration. One might argue that the idea of a comprehensive science plays the same role for structuralism as the notion of a comprehensive putting into question plays for some strains of so-called post-structuralism: neither a complete science nor a complete questioning is a possible accomplishment, but each is an imperative that produces telling analyses of the functioning of discourse. The notion that Barthes's work underwent a radical change in a move from structuralism to a post-structuralism in *S/Z* is an idea he helped to foster, but the concerns of *S/Z* were evident in his work all along. More palpable and significant is the shift that occurs when Barthes proclaims himself a hedonist.

Chapter 8
Hedonist

In 1975, explaining to an interviewer the importance the term *pleasure* had acquired in his work, Barthes spoke of his desire to 'take responsibility for a certain hedonism, the return of a discredited philosophy, repressed for centuries' (*Le Grain de la voix*, p. 195/206). *Le Plaisir du texte* is the primary document in this revival, but pleasure plays a prominent role in Barthes's other writings. 'What is an idea for him if not a *flush of pleasure* [*un empourprement de plaisir*]?' he asks in *Barthes par Barthes* (p. 107/103). 'The text is an object of pleasure,' he declares in *Sade/Fourier/Loyola* (p. 12/7). But pleasure must be *taken*. 'The challenge of literature is how can this work concern us, astonish us, fulfil us?'[19]

Le Plaisir du texte is a theory of textual pleasure, but also a manual and even a confession. 'What I enjoy in a story', Barthes reports, 'is not directly its content, nor even its structure, but the abrasions [*éraflures*] I impose on the fine surface: I speed ahead, I skip, I look up, I dip in again' (p. 22/11–12). Pleasure may come from *drifting* [*la dérive*], which 'occurs whenever *I do not respect the whole*' and he is carried along by language that seems opaque, theatrical, or even excessively precise (p. 32/18). He takes pleasure, for example, in 'exactitude': 'In *Bouvard et Pécuchet* I read this sentence, which gives me pleasure: "Cloths, sheets, napkins, were hanging vertically, attached by wooden clothespins to taut lines." Here I enjoy an excess of precision, a kind of maniacal exactitude of language, a descriptive madness (encountered in texts by Robbe-Grillet)' (p. 44/26). Recounting his pleasure in details of daily life in novels, biographies, or histories, Barthes goes on to imagine an aesthetics based on the pleasure of the consumer and 'a typology of the pleasures of reading – or of the readers of pleasure', in which each reading neurosis finds a particular textual pleasure: the fetishist is a lover of fragments, quotations, turns of phrase; the obsessional an enthusiastic manipulator of metalanguages, glosses, and explications; the paranoid a deep interpreter, seeker of secrets and complications; and the hysteric an enthusiast who abandons all critical detachment to throw himself into the text (pp. 99–100/63).

Discussions of reading and pleasure may seem to promote a mystique of the Text, but 'on the contrary,' Barthes insists, 'the whole effort consists in materializing the pleasure of the text, in making the text *an object of pleasure like any other* . . . The important thing is to equalize the field of pleasure, to abolish the false opposition of practical life and contemplative life. The pleasure of the text is just that: a claim lodged against the separation of the text' and an insistence on the extension of erotic investment to objects of all sorts, including languages and texts (p. 93/58–9).

To bring the text into the field of pleasure, Barthes invokes the body: 'The pleasure of the text is that moment when my body pursues its own ideas' (p. 30/17). Or again:

> Whenever I attempt to 'analyse' a text that has given me pleasure, it is not my 'subjectivity' I encounter but my 'individual', the given which makes my body separate from other bodies and appropriates suffering or pleasure to it: it is my enjoying body [*corps de jouissance*] I encounter. And this enjoying body is also *my historical subject*; for it is at the end of a very complex process combining biographical, historical, sociological and neurotic elements (education, social class, childhood configuration, etc.)

that I balance the contradictory interplay of (cultural) pleasure and (non-cultural) ecstasy.

Reference to the body is part of Barthes's general attempt to produce a materialist account of reading and writing, but it has four specific functions. First, the introduction of this unexpected term produces a salutary estrangement, especially in the French tradition, where the self has long been identified with consciousness, as in the Cartesian *cogito*, 'I think; therefore I am.' This self, a consciousness conscious of itself, is not what experiences textual pleasure: *the body* serves as Barthes's name for the entity involved – an entity altogether more opaque and heterogeneous, less in control and accessible to itself than the Cartesian 'mind'.

Second, structuralism has devoted much energy to demonstrating that the conscious subject should not be taken as a given and treated as the source of meaning but should rather be seen as the product of cultural forces and social codes that operate through it. For example, the conscious subject is not master of the language that it speaks. I 'know' English in the sense that my body can speak, write, and understand English, but I cannot bring to consciousness the vast and complex system of norms that constitute my knowledge. Noam Chomsky argues that we should not speak of children 'learning a language', as if this were an act of consciousness, but of language 'growing' in them. He calls language a 'mental organ', relating it to the body so as to stress that much more than consciousness is involved. Other cultural skills too entail much more than conscious knowledge: a connoisseur of wine cannot explain how to distinguish one year from another, but his body knows how to do it. Barthes's use of 'body' suggests considerations of this kind.

Third, given structuralism's treatment of the subject as the product of a host of codes and structural forces, my subjectivity, says Barthes in a passage from *S/Z* cited in Chapter 7, is only a faked plenitude, the wake of all the codes that constitute me – Barthes could not talk about the subject's pleasure without begging numerous questions he had insistently raised, yet he needs a way of speaking that takes account of the empirical fact that an individual can read and enjoy a text and that however stereotyped or generalized his subjectivity, certain experiences are best treated as his. The notion of the *body* permits Barthes to avoid the problem of the subject: appealing to 'the given that separates my body from other bodies and appropriates suffering or pleasure to it', he emphasizes that he is not talking about subjectivity. When a Russian cantor sings, 'the voice is not personal: it expresses nothing of the cantor, his soul; it is not original, and at the same time it is individual: it has us hear a body that has no identity, no "personality", but which is nevertheless a separate body' (*Image, Music, Text*, p. 182). *Le Roland-Barthes sans peine*, the parodic 'grammar' of Roland-Barthes, captures this theme quite nicely when it explains that in Roland-Barthes you recognize that you can't reach an agreement with someone by saying 'No doubt it's because you don't have the same body I do.'[20]

Fourth, replacement of 'mind' by 'body' accords with Barthes's emphasis on the materiality of the signifier as a source of pleasure. When listening to singing he prefers the corporeal 'grain of the voice' to expressiveness, meaning, or articulation. In Japan he delights in the opacity of Japanese culture for a foreigner (who does not see the meaning that would be obvious to a native). Everything he witnesses becomes a delightful display of bodily movement: 'There, the body exists' (*L'Empire des signes*, p. 20/10).

But despite these specific purposes, the appeal to the body seems to carry a constant possibility of mystification. Barthes's own formulations sometimes suggest that what comes from the body is deeper, truer, and above all more natural than anything else. 'I can do everything with my language *but not with my body*. What I hide by my language, my body

Doodling . . .

or the signifier without the signified

12. Doodling.

utters' (*Fragments d'un discours amoureux*, p. 54/44). Listen to a Russian cantor: 'something is there, manifest and stubborn, beyond (or before) the meaning of the words, something which is directly the cantor's *body*, brought into your ears from deep down in the cavities, the muscles, the membranes, the cartilages, and from deep down in the Slavonic language' (*Image, Music, Text*, p. 181). To maintain that an analysis of a text is based on the enjoying body is to claim considerable authenticity for it – more than if it were based on the sceptical mind. *Le Roland-Barthes sans peine* notes that when asked for the authority behind a statement, a speaker of Roland-Barthes should reply, 'I speak from my own body.' Barthes later confirms the astuteness of this analysis by beginning *La Chambre claire* with the question, 'What does my body know of Photography?' (p. 22/9) – a question whose presumption of the superiority of bodily knowledge invites the response, 'Even less than your mind.'

If, as often seems the case in Barthes's usage, 'body' is a stand-in for 'the subject', then the term offers a way of avoiding discussion of the unconscious and engagement with psychoanalysis, without sacrificing the appeal to a Nature more fundamental than conscious thought. When Barthes suggests that with any writer of past ages, 'there is a chance of "avant-garde" whenever it is the body and not ideology that writes' (*Le Grain de la voix*, p. 182/191), the invocation of the body suggests a natural substratum beyond the transient cultural features of a writer's ideas and initiates precisely the sort of mystification Barthes had analysed in 'The Family of Man', the exposition of photographs that tried to locate a Nature in human bodies beyond the superficial differences of cultural conditions and institutions.

Barthes is quite aware of the mystification that can accompany appeals to the body (or to Desire, which also functioned as a new name for Nature in recent French thought). *Image, Music, Text* notes that the notion of organic totality, 'which must be fractured', gains much of its mystificatory power from its implicit reference to the body as the image of a unified totality (p. 174). *Barthes par Barthes* identifies *corps* as his 'mana-word': 'a word whose ardent, complex, ineffable, and somehow sacred signification gives the illusion that this word holds an answer to everything' (p. 133/129). But in his new hedonism, Barthes was unwilling to give up either the term or the implicit reference to Nature that it constantly brought into his writing. He who once mercilessly exposed the bourgeois attempt to substitute Nature for culture, and to eliminate intellect while relying on what is directly 'felt' or goes-without-saying, could now write, for example: 'I can hear with certainty – the certainty of the body, of thrill – that the harpsichord playing of Wanda Landowska comes from her inner body and not from the petty digital scramble of so many harpsichordists (so much so that it is a different instrument)' (*Image, Music, Text*, p. 189). Is this a different Barthes?

In fact, aside from the strategic functions I have mentioned, appeal to the body has little explanatory power. In *La Chambre claire*, asking 'What does my body know of Photography?', Barthes discovers only that certain photographs 'existed for me'. He had then to 'posit a structural rule', which is a rule of contrast: a photograph's *studium*, as he names it, is what one perceives by virtue of one's general culture and understanding of the world – an understanding of what is represented – while its *punctum* is something that punctuates or disturbs that scene, 'that accident which pricks me' (pp. 44–9/23–7). 'I had to grant', Barthes concludes, 'that my desire was an imperfect mediator, and that a subjectivity reduced to its hedonistic project could not recognize the universal' (p. 95/60). (In the second part of the book he goes on to relate photography to the general forces of love and death.)

Le Plaisir du texte, despite its repeated reference to corporeal pleasure, is also a theoretical work. It transforms *S/Z*'s distinction between the readerly and the writerly into an asymmetrical opposition between two kinds of pleasure, *plaisir* and *jouissance*. Sometimes *pleasure* is the general term for reading pleasures of all sorts. 'On the one hand, I need a general "pleasure" whenever I must refer to an excess of the text . . .

and on the other hand, I need a particular "pleasure", a simple part of Pleasure as a whole, whenever I need to distinguish euphoria, fulfillment, comfort (the feeling of repletion when culture penetrates freely), from shock, disruption, even loss, which are proper to ecstasy' (p. 34/19). At times, Barthes insists upon the distinction: the text of pleasure is the readerly text, one we know how to read; the text of ecstasy (*jouissance*, unfortunately rendered as 'bliss' by the translator) is 'the text that imposes a state of loss, that discomforts (perhaps to the point of a certain boredom), unsettles the reader's historical, cultural, psychological assumptions, the consistency of his tastes, values, memories, brings to a crisis his relation with language' (pp. 25–6/14).

The book explores the relations (historical, psychological; typological) between these two sorts of text or aspects of texts and, while maintaining the importance of a distinction, seems frequently to suggest that textual pleasure and textual effects depend upon the possibility of finding ecstatic moments in the comfortable texts of pleasure or of making ecstatic post-modern writing sufficiently readable that its disruptive, violent, orgasmic effects can be generated. 'Neither culture nor its destruction is erotic,' Barthes writes, 'it is the gap between them that becomes so . . . it is not violence that impresses pleasure; destruction does not interest it; what it desires is the site of a loss, a seam, a cut, a deflation, the *dissolve* that seizes the reader at the moment of ecstasy' (p. 15/7). A naked body is less erotic than the spot 'where the garment leaves gaps' (p. 19/9). Avant-garde techniques, or disruptions of traditional expectations, are more pleasurably startling as gaps in a readable discourse: Flaubert, for example, has 'a way of cutting, of perforating discourse, without rendering it meaningless' (p. 18/8). 'The text needs its shadow, a *bit* of ideology, a *bit* of representation, a *bit* of subject: ghosts, pockets, traces, necessary clouds: subversion must produce its own *chiaroscuro*' (p. 53/32). Even so, discontinuities, dissolves, indeterminacies, and moments of unreadability imply, Barthes says, a certain boredom. 'Boredom is not far from ecstasy,' he suggests, 'it is ecstasy viewed from the shores of pleasure' (p. 43/25–6). 'There is no *sincere* boredom' – it is only ecstasy approached with other requirements.

This maxim on boredom illustrates what Barthes is doing in *Le Plaisir du texte*. We usually think of boredom as an immediate affective experience, but it is a major theoretical category with a role in any theory of reading. If one reads intently every word of a Zola novel, one becomes bored, as one does if one tries to skim through *Finnegans Wake* for the plot. To reflect on boredom is to think about texts and the strategies of reading they require, an enterprise more theoretical than confessional. If *Le Plaisir du texte* seems not to take itself seriously as theory, self-consciously avoiding continuity, this does not mean that readers should not take it seriously, as fragments of a continuing theoretical enterprise.

Barthes's revival of hedonism may be his most difficult project to assess, for it seems to indulge in some of the mystifications he had effectively exposed, yet it continues to challenge intellectual orthodoxy. Talk of pleasure had been set aside as irrelevant by the most powerful intellectual enterprises of the day, especially those he had encouraged, so that his promotion of hedonism was a radical step. But his celebrations of the pleasure of the text seemed to point literary criticism towards values the traditionalists had never abandoned, and his references to bodily pleasures created for many a new Barthes, less forbiddingly scientific or intellectual. His distinctive revolt against an intellectual climate he had helped to create made him in certain ways palatable to a broad public, who could now see in him a familiar figure: the sensitive, self-indulgent man of letters, who writes about his own interests and pleasures without in any way challenging fundamental ways of thinking. Strategic and radical in certain ways, Barthes's hedonism repeatedly exposes him to charges of complacency. *Sollers écrivain* speaks of the central pleasure afforded by 'the passage of sensual objects into discourse', which may save the most severe writing from boredom. Sollers's work '*H* is a forest of words, within which I seek

13. Roland Barthes with Marie-France Pisier, playing the role of Thackeray in André Téchiné's film *Les Sœurs Brontë*.

what will *touch* me (when we were children we used to hunt in the countryside for chocolate eggs that had been hidden there) . . . I await the fragment that will concern me and establish *meaning for me*' (p. 58/77). That parenthesis, in all its sentimental bathos, may be one of Barthes's most daring moments as a writer, but it is one readers should approach with some wariness.

Chapter 9
Writer

When Barthes looks back on his work in *Barthes par Barthes*, he sees not a critic nor a semiologist but a writer. He does not weigh the validity of the concepts he has stressed but notes their efficacy as tactics of writing: they 'make the text go', they 'permit him to say something'. The death of his mother made him want to write about her, and his final course of lectures at the Collège de France, on 'Preparation for the Novel', showed a surprising interest in details of writers' lives: how they organized their time, their work spaces, and their social lives while writing. In interviews and in *Barthes par Barthes*, he discussed his own 'relation with the instruments of writing' (fountain pen preferred to ballpoint or typewriter) and the organization of his desk and daily schedule – discussions nicely parodied in *Le Roland-Barthes sans peine*. For the true writer, he had once declared, *to write* is an intransitive verb: one does not write *something*, one simply writes.[21] Now, he presents his own work in these terms: his vocation is not analysing particular sorts of phenomena but *writing*. *Barthes par Barthes* is not criticism of his past works: 'I abandon the exhausting pursuit of an old piece of myself, I do not try to *restore* myself (as we say of a monument). I do not say: "I am going to describe myself"; but: "I am writing a text, and I call it R.B." ' (p. 60/56). He suggests that all his work may be a clandestine attempt to revive the Gidean journal, a literary form whose fragments self-reflexively explore the writer's engagement with writing.

Even at the time when he was proposing new sciences, he gave himself the writer's licence to steal and exploit the language of other disciplines. 'Myth Today' in *Mythologies* tells us in its first paragraph that Myth is 'a type of speech', 'a system of communication', 'a message', and 'a mode of signification', blithely disregarding the important distinctions among these terms in linguistics. Later, his writerly relation to concepts becomes more pronounced and a subject for comment. *La Chambre claire*, he says, starts from 'a vague, casual, even cynical phenomenology, so readily did it agree to distort or to evade its principles according to the whim of my analysis' (p. 40/20). A fragment of *Barthes par Barthes* describes this propensity in different terms:

> In relation to the systems which surround him, what is he? Say an echo chamber: he reproduces the thoughts badly, he follows the words, he pays his visits, i.e., his respects, to vocabularies, he *invokes* notions, he rehearses them under a name; he makes use of this name as of an emblem (thereby practising a kind of philosophical ideography) and this emblem dispenses him from following to its conclusion the system of which it is the signifier (which simply makes a sign to him). Coming from psychoanalysis and seeming to remain there, '*transference*' nonetheless readily leaves the Oedipal situation. The Lacanian '*image-repertory*' [*imaginaire*] extends to the borders of the classical 'self-love' [*amour-propre*] ... '*Bourgeois*' receives the whole Marxist accent, but keeps overflowing toward the aesthetic and the ethical. In this way, no doubt, words are shifted, systems communicate, modernity is tried (the way one tries all the push buttons on a radio one doesn't know how to work), but the intertext thereby created is literally *superficial*: one adheres *loosely*: the name (philosophic, psychoanalytic, political, scientific) retains with its original system a line which is not cut but remains: tenacious and floating. No doubt the reason for this is that one cannot at one and the same time desire a word and take it to its conclusion: in him the desire for the word prevails, but this pleasure is partly constituted by a kind of doctrinal vibration.

p. 78/74

88

Whatever the pleasures of liberating a term from its original system, the 'doctrinal vibration' has been important to the success of Barthes's writings, and when he gives that up by inventing his own terms, abandoning the suggestive support of another body of discourse, the effects are quite different. Always a lover of classifications, he used to draw upon technical terms or Greek coinages. In *Sur Racine* he maintained that there were three sorts of literary history: a history of literary signifieds, a history of literary signifiers, and a history of literary signification. The use of terms that belong together and are sustained by a system of thought gives the typology a logic and a plausibility, even if the terms are applied figuratively. Consider by contrast a typology from *Sollers écrivain*, where Barthes suggests that there are five ways of reading Sollers: '*en piqué*', '*en prisé*', '*en déroulé*', '*en rase-mottes*', and '*en plein-ciel*', which might be crudely rendered as 'in spearing', 'in savouring', 'in unrolling', 'in nose-to-the-ground', and 'in full-horizon' (pp. 75–6/89–90). This typology is doubly figurative: the categories are presented as if they were modes or keys (a reading '*in* full-horizon'), and they are drawn from quite different areas of discourse. They have little in common and apply in oblique ways to reading. To read 'in the spearing mode' is to pick out flavourful phrases here and there; to read 'in the savouring mode' is to take in fully a particular development; to read 'in the unrolling mode' is to proceed swiftly and evenly, while a 'nose-to-the-ground reading' progresses word by word, and a 'full-horizon' reading takes overviews, seeing the text as an object in context. This is what one might call a disposable typology: suggestive, perhaps witty, but with no theoretical claims and little chance that others will try to integrate it in a theory of reading. Barthes continued to make theoretical statements but increasingly found ways of presenting them that undermine their theoretical status.

As a writer he is distinctive and formidable: a master of French prose who forged a new and livelier language for intellectual discussion. Opting for an unusually loose, appositional syntax which strings together phrases or clauses that come at a phenomenon from different angles, he manages to give a sensuous concreteness to abstract concepts. The basis of his art is the application of a term and suggestions of its usual context to a quite different context, perhaps most noticeable in the metaphors where the transported context is made explicit: 'I do not restore myself (as we say of a monument)'; 'exempt from meaning (as one is from military service)'. Barthes describes his imagination as 'homological' rather than metaphorical, given to comparing systems rather than particular objects (*Barthes par Barthes*, p. 62/58). This is both a feature of his style and a general analytical strategy, as when he treats some activity as a language and seeks out the possible constituents and distinctions this entails.

L'Empire des signes is his first work not tied to a critical, analytical project. Japan, he observed, 'liberated me considerably on the plane of writing' (*Le Grain de la voix*, p. 217/229). He found before him in daily life objects and practices which provoked euphoric writing, a happy *Mythologies* of a civilization contrary to our own. Instead of imagining a fictional utopia, he wrote, '[I can] without claiming in any way to depict or analyse any reality whatsoever, select from somewhere in the world a number of features (a graphic and linguistic term) and from them form a system. It is this system that I shall call "Japan"' (p. 93/71). Twenty-six long fragments reflecting on some aspect of this culture – food, theatre, faces, elaborate packages with nothing of consequence inside, haiku, slot machines – sketch Barthes's utopia, where artifice reigns, forms are emptied of meaning, and all is surface. The capitalist Japan of economic miracles and technological supremacy makes no appearance, but Barthes knew what a transgression he was committing in idealizing Japan at a time when his friends at the journal *Tel Quel* were promoting Mao Zedong and China's Cultural Revolution. Whatever its reality, Japan put Barthes '*en situation d'écriture*' (in a writing situation).

Barthes par Barthes is perhaps this writer's most remarkable performance. A collection of fragments alphabetically arranged, some in the first person and some in the third, and with rather contingent titles that may have been added afterwards to suggest an arbitrary order, this is 'not the book of his ideas' but 'the book of his resistance to his own ideas' (p. 123/119). Seductive in its imaginative self-deprecation, it tempts one to use it as an authoritative guide, especially since it denies its own authority: 'What I write about myself is never *the last word*: the more "sincere" I am, the more interpretable I am . . . my texts are disjointed, no one of them caps any other; the latter is nothing but a *further* text, the last of the series, not the ultimate in meaning: *text upon text*, which never illuminates anything' (p. 124/120).

He resists his ideas and he talks about 'R.B.', not analysing himself but 'staging an image-system' – moving around images of himself like flats on a stage, bringing some in from the wings, moving others back, arranging them. He offers childhood memories, more positive and nostalgic than his previous remarks about his life lead one to expect. He does not hesitate to sketch the peaceful, middle-class existence that he leads, especially when vacationing in the country, and suggests that 'it is certainly when I divulge my private life the most that I expose myself the most', for by the *Doxa* of a left-wing intelligentsia, what is truly 'private', disreputable, 'is trivial actions, the traces of bourgeois ideology confessed by the subject' (p. 85/82). In these terms he does indeed take risks, though the book is surprisingly reticent on other matters. He writes of his mother but never even mentions his half-brother, whom some obscure motive systematically excludes from his writing, as though his imagination required that the mother be there for him alone. And this proponent of the body commits no sexual indiscretions. A fragment on 'The Goddess H.' remarks that 'the pleasure potential of a perversion (in this case, that of the two H.s, homosexuality and hashish) is always underestimated' (p. 68/63), but no avowal or anecdote indicates what his sexual life had been. It remained for posthumous texts, particularly *Incidents*, to reveal an unhappy homosexual existence: hours of thinking about young men but declining to act; disappointment in those encounters that are reported. In 'writing the self, in collecting the image system, I tie it up in order to protect myself and at the same time to offer myself' (p. 166/162). The proportions are carefully calculated.

Barthes's qualities may be best displayed in fragments like the following, a self-conscious reflection upon writing:

> An aphoristic tone hangs about this book (*we, one, always*). Now the maxim is complicitous with an essentialist notion of human nature; it is linked to classical ideology: it is the most arrogant (often the stupidest) of the forms of language. Why then not reject it? The reason is, as always, emotive: I write maxims (or I sketch their movement) *in order to reassure myself*: when some disturbance arises, I attenuate it by confiding myself to a fixity which exceeds my powers: 'Actually, it's always like that': and the maxim is born. The maxim is a sort of *sentence-name*, and to name is to pacify. Moreover, this too is a maxim: it attenuates my fear of seeking extravagance by writing maxims.
>
> *Barthes par Barthes*, p. 181/17

The force of such reflections depends on their identification of emotional causes for intellectual constructions: they appeal as though seeking an explanation of the world. But since what seduces is a forceful explanation – an intellectual construct – the reader, like the author himself, is trapped in a discursive circle. The more credence one gives to this reflection, the more one must suspect it. Such entrapments are the effects of powerful writing.

Barthes's most popular and unusual performance as a writer is *Fragments d'un discours amoureux*, a writing out of the discourse of love. This language – primarily the complaints and reflections of the lover when alone, not exchanges of a lover with his or her partner – is unfashionable. Though it is spoken by millions of people, diffused in our popular romances and television programmes as well as in serious literature, there is no institution that explores, maintains, modifies, judges, repeats, and otherwise assumes responsibility for this discourse.

14. 'Peter is completely fictitious, but he's extremely well written.'

Taking on something of this role, Barthes finds in it a way of producing 'the novelistic': the novel minus plot and characters. Under headings alphabetically arranged, from *s'abîmer* (to be engulfed) to *vouloir-saisir* (will-to-possess), Barthes puts together discourse of various kinds: quotations and paraphrases from literary works, especially Goethe's *The Sorrows of Young Werther*, first-person statements in which an unnamed lover reflects on and gives voice to his situation, and ruminations suggested by various theoretical writings (Plato, Nietzsche, Lacan). The series of fragments or 'figures', as he calls them ('figures' in the sense of 'poses'), presents the material for a novel, a multitude of scenes and passionate or reflective utterances, and there are tantalizing hints of a personal love story, but there is no development or continuity, no plot or progress in a love relation, and, instead of developing characters, only the generalized roles of the lover and the loved one.

The headings are the names of amorous 'numbers' or 'turns':

> If there is such a figure as 'Anxiety', it is because the subject sometimes exclaims (without any concern for the clinical sense of the word): 'Je suis angoissé' (I am having an anxiety attack!) *'Angoscia!'* Callas sings somewhere. The figure is a kind of operatic aria; just as this aria is identified, memorized and manipulated through its *incipit* ('When I am laid', *'Pleurez, mes yeux'*, *'Lucevan le stelle'*, *'Piangerò la mia sorte')*, so the figure takes its departure from a turn of phrase, a kind of verse, refrain or cantillation, which articulates it in the darkness.

p. 9/5

'I want to understand . . .', 'What is to be done . . .?', 'When my finger accidentally . . .', 'This can't go on . . .' are some of the *incipits* of Barthes's amorous figures, introducing fragments which, he says, we will *recognize.* 'Figures take shape insofar as we can recognize, in passing discourse, something that has been read, heard, felt' (p. 8/4). As a grammar of a language is a description of native speakers' linguistic competence and seeks to capture what is grammatically acceptable to speakers of the language, so Barthes attempts to capture what is acceptable, recognizable, according to the codes and stereotypes of our culture, as a lover's complaint. Goethe's *Werther* he takes as a reference point since it has served as a model of amorous attitudes for so much of European culture and provides a rich lode of this complex sentimental, neglected rhetoric.

Barthes proposes to simulate this discourse, not to analyse it, but moments of analysis frequently emerge, and the simulated lover proves himself to be a skilled analyst, reflecting intensely on his condition and on the signs that surround him. Consider 'Quand mon doigt par mégarde . . .' (When my finger accidentally . . .). 'The figure refers to any interior discourse provoked by furtive contact with the body (and more precisely the skin) of the desired being.' One might expect the lover to concentrate on the physical delight of bodily contact, but he is in love: he creates meaning everywhere, out of nothing, and it is meaning that thrills him: he is in the crucible of meaning. Every contact, for the lover, raises the question of the response: the skin is asked to reply.

(A squeeze of the hand – an immense dossier of information – a tiny gesture within the palm, a knee which doesn't move away, an arm extended, as if quite naturally, along the back of a sofa and against which the other's head gradually comes to rest – this is the paradisic realm of subtle and clandestine signs: like a festival, not of the senses but of meaning.)

p. 81/67

The lover lives in a universe of signs: nothing involving the beloved is without meaning, and he can spend hours classifying and interpreting the details of behaviour. 'The incident is trivial (it is always trivial) but it will attract to it whatever language I possess' (p. 83/69).

Barthes is resourceful and convincing in describing the lover's semiotic deliberations. Frequently, a lover finds himself caught up in the 'deliberative figure' of 'What is to be done?':

My anxieties about behaviour are futile, ever more so, to infinity. If the other, incidentally or negligently, gives the telephone number of a place where he or she can be reached at certain times, I immediately grow baffled: should I telephone or shouldn't I? (It would do no good to tell me that I *can* telephone – that is the objective, reasonable meaning of the message – for it is precisely this *permission* I don't know how to handle.)

. . . for me, an amorous subject, everything that is new, everything that disturbs, is received not as a fact but as a sign that must be interpreted. From the lover's point of view, the fact becomes consequential because it is immediately transformed into a sign: it is the sign, not the fact, that is consequential (by its reverberations). If the other has given me this new telephone number, what was that the sign of? Was it an invitation to telephone *right away*, for the pleasure of the call, or only *should the occasion arise*, out of necessity? My answer itself will be a sign, which the other will inevitably interpret, thereby releasing, between us, a tumultuous manoeuvring of images. *Everything signifies*: by this proposition, I entrap myself, I bind myself in calculations, I keep myself from enjoyment.

Sometimes, by dint of deliberating about 'nothing' (as the world sees it), I exhaust myself; then I try, in reaction, to return – like a drowning man who stamps on the floor of the sea – to a *spontaneous* decision (spontaneity: the great dream: paradise, power, ecstasy): *go on, telephone, since you want to!* But such recourse is futile: amorous time does not permit the subject to align impulse and action, to make them coincide: I am not the man of mere 'acting out' – my madness is tempered, it is not seen; it is *right away* that I fear consequences, any consequence: it is my fear – my deliberation – which is 'spontaneous'.

pp. 75–6/62–3

Such novelistic fragments not only portray recognizable figures of lovers' thought but vividly display mechanisms of signification and their entrammelling complications. What distinguishes the lover, obsessive interpreter and clear-sighted analyst of his interpretive predicament, from the semiologist or mythologist is the sentimentality of his discourse: he mistakes conventional signs for motivated signs, investing the trivial objects that surround him with special meaning seen as inherent, intrinsic.[22] This sentimentality, 'discredited by modern opinion', makes love unfashionable, even 'obscene', a topic not to be discussed in polite company – unlike sex, which is accepted as an important subject of current discourse. '(Historical reversal: it is no longer the *sexual* which is indecent, it is the *sentimental* – censured in the name of what is finally only *another morality*)' (p. 209/177). But the true 'obscenity' of love's sentimentality lies in the fact that one cannot, by publishing sentimentality, commit a dramatic transgression, so that

Barthes

it remains completely beyond the pale. 'The obscenity of love is extreme. Nothing can redeem it, bestow upon it the positive value of a transgression . . . The amorous text (scarcely a text at all) consists of petty narcissisms, psychological paltrinesses; it is without grandeur: or its grandeur . . . is to be unable to attain grandeur' (p. 211/178–9).

Barthes, promoter of the Marquis de Sade, had worked to create an intellectual climate attuned to transgression. To bring back the sentimentality of ordinary love, he suggests, is a transgression of transgression, a violation of the orthodoxy that values radical transgression. Writing out the figures of a neglected discourse, Barthes surprises us in *Fragments* by making love, in its most absurd and sentimental forms, not only engaging in a novelistic way but an object of considerable semiological interest.

Chapter 10
Man of letters

'I have no biography,' Barthes declares. 'Or, rather, since the time of the first line I wrote, I no longer see myself.' He can and does recall his childhood and recount his adolescence, but since then, 'everything happens through writing' (*Le Grain de la voix*, p. 245/259). His acute, self-deprecatory reflections on the self present him as a miscellany of ideas, declarations, and propositions, an unstable collection of fragments with no unity or centre: 'the subject that I am is not unified' (p. 283/304). *Barthes par Barthes* alternates between two views. On the one hand, it complains that 'writing the self' threatens to displace the self by fictions. 'Freewheeling in language, I have nothing to compare myself to; . . . the symbol becomes literally *immediate*; essential danger for the life of the subject: to write on oneself may seem a pretentious idea; but it is also a simple idea: simple as the idea of suicide' (p. 62/56). But on the other hand, these fragments also conclude that there is nothing behind these fictions: the self is a discursive construction; 'the subject is merely an effect of language,' a self of letters (p. 82/79). 'Do I not know that, *in the field of the subject, there is no referent?* . . . I am the story which happens to me' (p. 60/56). For himself, as for us, Barthes is a collection of writings, whose contrasts or contradictions cannot be eliminated by determining which formulations or propositions are truly 'Barthes's' – except insofar as 'Barthes' is itself a construction formed to order these fragments.

Barthes is a man of letters in the sense that his life is a life of writing, an adventure with language; but by the end of his life he had come to occupy the role of man of letters in a traditional sense. He seemed to have become an embodiment of 'literary values': a love for language, particularly the well-turned phrase or richly suggestive image, a sensitivity to the psychological suggestiveness of objects and events, an interest in cultural productions of all sorts, and a commitment to the primacy of the mental life. He was not just a critic, but a literary figure whose pronouncements on cultural issues represented, for his contemporaries, a cultured, aesthetic attitude. When he spoke to a reporter about laziness – one of his last interviews was entitled 'Dare to be Lazy!' – he could be relied on to provide elegant, unorthodox formulations, enlivened by a theoretical perspective, with insightful discriminations and a concern for spiritual values. He regularly wrote prefaces to new books or exhibition catalogues, discussed food, going to the opera, playing the piano, remembering childhood.[23] In *Leçon* he claims that 'the myth of the Great French Writer, the sacred depositary of all higher values, has crumbled,' and a new type has appeared, 'whom we no longer know – or do not yet know – how to name: writer? intellectual? scriptor? In any event, literary *mastery* is disappearing. The writer is no longer centre stage' (p. 40/475). Barthes might be this new type, achieving authority through his relinquishment of mastery, proposing 'excursions': fragments that explore, through the theoretical languages of our day, experiences of thinking and living.

La Chambre claire, his last book, shows him in the role of cultural commentator. Eschewing technical knowledge and thus emphasizing that he brings to his reflection on photographs only his literary culture, his sensitivity, and his human experience, he decides to 'derive all photography' from one photograph of his mother which, for him, represents her 'changed into herself'. Positing photography's connections with love and death, he eloquently and sensitively explores his responses to his mother's recent death: 'For what I have lost is not a Figure (the Mother), but a being, and not a being but a *quality* (a soul):

not the indispensable, but the irreplaceable. I could live without the Mother (as we all do, sooner or later); but what life remained would be absolutely and entirely *unqualifiable* (without qualities)' (p. 118/75).

Photographs, he concludes, say 'this has been'; 'the photograph's essence is to ratify what it represents' (p. 133/85). The appeal of this mode of writing, in which Barthes embodies in an unthreatening way the 'wisdom' or insight a literary sensibility might achieve, emerges in the review in *Newsweek*, which praises the lyrical humanism of this 'great book': 'Barthes takes the reader on an exquisitely rendered, lyrical journey into the heart of his own life and the medium he came to love, a medium that flirts constantly with the "intractable reality" of the human condition.'

How did Roland Barthes, the critic of bourgeois myth, reach this point? In *Barthes par Barthes* he describes a mechanism and proposes a trajectory:

> Reactive formations: a *Doxa* (a popular opinion) is posited, intolerable; to free myself from it, I postulate a paradox; then this paradox turns bad, becomes a new concretion, itself becomes a new *Doxa*, and I must seek further for a new paradox.

> Let us follow this trajectory. At the work's source, the opacity of social relations, a false Nature; the first thrust, then, is to demystify (*Mythologies*); then, when the demystification is immobilized in repetition, it must be displaced: semiological *science* (then postulated) tries to stir, to vivify, to arm the mythological gesture, or pose, by endowing it with a method; this science is encumbered in its turn by a whole repertoire of images: the goal of a semiological science is replaced by the (often very grim) science of the semiologists; hence, one must sever oneself from that, must introduce into this rational image-repertoire the texture of desire, the claims of the body: this, then, is the

15. Barthes at piano.

Text, the theory of the Text. But again the Text risks paralysis: it repeats itself, counterfeits itself in lustreless texts ... the Text tends to degenerate into prattle (*Babil*). Where to go next? That is where I am now.

p. 75/71

In a first stage, he seeks to reform signs: *Larvatus prodeo* (I advance pointing to my mask) is repeatedly proposed (three times in *Le Degré zéro* alone) as the ideal motto for signifying activities. A science of signs seems the way to bring together what he sees as the most interesting strands of contemporary research: 'psychoanalysis, structuralism, eidetic psychology, some new types of literary criticism of which Bachelard has given the first examples, are no longer concerned with facts except inasmuch as they are endowed with significance. Now to postulate a signification is to have recourse to semiology' (*Mythologies*, pp. 195-6/111). But once the programme for a semiology is established, Barthes's reaction made his work something of an 'unwriting' of

Intertext	Genre	Works
(Gide)	(desire to write)	–
Sartre Marx Brecht	social mythology	*Writing Degree Zero* Writings on theater *Mythologies*
Saussure	semiology	*Elements of Semiology* *Système de la mode*
Sollers, Kristeva Derrida, Lacan	textuality	*S/Z* *Sade, Fourier, Loyola* *L'Empire des signes*
(Nietzsche)	morality	*The Pleasure of the Text* *Roland Barthes by Roland Barthes*

16. Intertext/Genre/Works diagram.

science. The metalanguages he had sought to establish were now treated as givens; to 'loosen' theory he takes over their terms, severing them from all but a few of their defining distinctions, encouraging them to drift into other relations. The *text*, one of his 'mana-words', came to represent an unmasterable object, an endless perspective of signifying relations. Woven of prior discourses, the text is ultimately related to all of culture. The notion of the reader joined that of the text to form an unmasterable couple: against any attempt to master the text through analysis, one could emphasize the vital role of the reader – no meaning or structure except what the reader produces. But against any attempt to make the reader the object of a (psychological) science, one could emphasize that texts have the resources to disrupt readers' most assured presumptions and to disappoint their most authoritative strategies.

A striking feature of Barthes's accounts of literature since *S/Z* is how easily reader and text switch places in the stories he tells: the story of the reader structuring a text flips over into a story of the text manipulating the reader. In the entry on 'Texte, theorie du' for the *Encyclopaedia universalis*, he writes that 'the signifier belongs to everyone,' but, he quickly continues, 'it is the text which works untiringly, not the artist or the consumer'. On the next page he reverts to the first position: 'the theory of the text removes all limits to the freedom of reading (authorizing the reading of a past work from an entirely modern standpoint . . .) but it also insists greatly on the productive equivalence of reading and writing'. Celebration of the reader as the producer of the text is matched by description of the text as the controlling force in these encounters. The result is to focus attention on this interaction while preventing the adoption of a point of view that would encourage systematic investigation.[24]

The turn in Barthes's writing to the body and to the pleasures of daily life seems a significant displacement. At the very least, the subjects and mode of writing of this new phase made Barthes newly palatable to the bourgeoisie he had once attacked. The new words 'pleasure', 'charm' and 'wisdom' made intelligence less threatening, and the new topics – the sorrows of love, childhood memories, maternal devotion and scenes of provincial life – encouraged the French public to discover Barthes as a writer. Who would have imagined that the Roland Barthes who had presided over 'the death of the author', as he called it, would now lecture at the Collège de France on the habits of classic French authors (Balzac's dressing gown, Flaubert's notebooks, Proust's cork-lined room), and would describe his own works not as contributions to this or that general enterprise, but as manifestations of his own desire? We might reach for his favourite figure, the spiral, to describe this strange recurrence: attitudes previously rejected reappear in his writing, but in another place, at a different level. As he declares his opposition to all systems, he strangely resembles the literary traditionalists who spurned the young Roland Barthes as an insensitive reductionist. In *La Chambre claire* he declares that 'the only sure thing in me is 'a desperate resistance to any reductive system' (p. 21/8) and seems to forget the strategic function of systems in preventing one from falling back into the unperceived, 'natural' stereotypes of one's culture.

Barthes, of course, notes his bringing back of topics and attitudes dear to the cultural tradition he had once tried to alter, but he sees this as another transgression, a disruption of intellectuals' orthodoxy. 'To reintroduce into the domain of politico-sexual discourse that has been opened up, recognized, liberated, explored . . . a *touch of sentimentality*: would that not be the ultimate transgression?' (*Barthes par Barthes*, p. 70/66). One can indeed view Barthes's work as creating a climate in which it can then reintroduce the traditional as an avant-garde transgression, but there are several problems that encourage scepticism about the radical nature of his final phase.

First, there is the ease with which Nature slips back into his writing: above all in the guise of the body, but also as the 'intractable referent' in photography, what is simply *there*, authoritative and indubitable. Barthes's critical and analytical work repeatedly exposed attempts to posit a Nature beneath culture and to adduce a natural ground for one's actions and interpretations. In later years, though, he falls increasingly prey to what seems to be a law of discourse: when you expose Nature as culture and banish it from one place, it reappears elsewhere.

Secondly, Barthes profits from the systematic endeavours he renounces, and one could accept these renunciations with better grace if he were more ready to recognize his profits. His success as a writer of fragments could not have occurred if his brief reflections were not connected in myriad ways – by their vocabulary, by their explicit topics – with the systematic enterprises that had made his reputation. The reflections in *Barthes par Barthes* are provocative precisely because familiar terms are being used in new ways – to loosen the theories they once helped to build. Barthes's work has always been incomplete: he offers projects, outlines, visions. He is irritating when he presents incompleteness as a virtue, as in *S/Z*, where further investigation of codes would in fact strengthen a Barthesian analysis. The dislike of system in the late works is certainly a resistance to authority but can also be interpreted as self-serving and complacent – as if his account of laziness as resistance to authority had led him to follow his own advice: 'Dare to be lazy!'

Thirdly, Barthes's writings increasingly promote what seems a powerful myth, the myth of 'exemption from meaning'. In *Barthes par Barthes* he writes, 'Obviously he dreams of a world which would be *exempt from meaning* (as one is exempt from military service). This began with *Writing Degree Zero*, which imagines "the absence of every sign"; subsequently, a thousand affirmations incidental to this dream (apropos of the avant-garde text, of Japan, of music, of the alexandrine, etc.)' (p. 90/87). Always there is the dream not of meaninglessness but of forms with empty meaning. As a critical notion, this has a crucial strategic role – among other things, it encourages a poetics that seeks to understand forms rather than a hermeneutics that seeks meaning – but in Barthes's later works he begins to present as a transgression what could easily be taken as a reaffirmation of quite regressive, pre-semiological notions. Photographs, he claims, simply represent what has been: he recalls a photograph of a slave in which 'slavery was given without mediation, the fact was established without method' (p. 125/80). This is precisely the alibi of another photograph analysed in *Mythologies*, the photograph of the black soldier saluting the French flag, whose pretence of unmediated representation (the *alibi* that in fact black soldiers who salute the French flag do exist) Barthes was swift to dismiss and whose insertion in the ideological systems of French culture he easily demonstrated.

Barthes senses that there is a problem here. The fragment 'Exemption from Meaning' continues, 'Curious that in public opinion, precisely, there should be a version of this dream; the Doxa, too, has no love for meaning . . . it counters the invasion of meaning (for which intellectuals are responsible) with the *concrete*; the concrete is what is supposed to resist meaning.' But perhaps this is not so curious; perhaps it is much the same myth in both cases, despite the eloquent expression it acquires as it spirals back in Barthes's work. He maintains that he is not repeating this myth: he does not seek a condition *prior* to meaning but imagines one *beyond* meaning (an *après-sens*): 'one must traverse, as though the length of an initiatic way, the whole meaning, in order to be able to extenuate it, to exempt it.' This difference is marked in most of his writings about literature, but when he turns to photography he imagines not an emptying out of meaning or a disturbance of cultural codes, but states that are simply *there*, prior to meaning. Defying all the most convincing work on meaning, including and perhaps especially his own, he reaffirms the powerful myth he taught us to resist. Perhaps, though, we should not be surprised that the semiologist who showed us that we never escape meaning should be increasingly tempted to find some natural spot that escapes cultural codes.

Among the many things that return, but in another place, is traditional literature of the 19th century. Barthes began as the champion of experimental literature – Flaubert, Camus, Robbe-Grillet – but the comfortable, intelligible literature that he set aside for its failure to experiment with language or take a critical stance to the codes on which it relies returned as his first love and as the main subject of his teaching at the Collège de France. His whole project might even be conceived as a roundabout way of breaking the academy's hold on 19th-century literature, so that it could be brought back, not as an object of knowledge or of study, but as an object of pleasure, as a source of transgressions without grandeur. By taking avant-garde literature as the model, *S/Z* and *Le Plaisir du texte* elaborate a practice of reading which can reveal the excesses, the complications, and the subversions of Balzac, Chateaubriand, Proust. *Fragments d'un discours amoureux* makes the sentimental and unfashionable discourse of *Werther* an object of contemporary interest. This is no mean accomplishment, and is made possible by the theoretical arguments that broke traditional criticism's hold on literature. An eloquent passage of *Leçon*, worth citing in French, explains:

> *Les valeurs anciennes ne se transmettent plus, ne circulent plus, n'impressionnent plus; la littérature est désacralisée, les institutions sont impuissantes à la protéger et à l'imposer comme le modèle implicite de l'humain. Ce n'est pas, si l'on veut, que la littérature soit détruite; c'est qu'elle n'est plus gardée: c'est donc le moment d'y aller. La sémiologie littéraire serait ce voyage qui permet de débarquer dans un paysage libre par déshérence: ni anges ni dragons ne sont plus là pour le défendre; le regard peut alors se porter, non sans perversité; sur des choses anciennes et belles, dont le signifié est abstrait, périmé: moment à la fois decadent et prophétique, moment d'apocalypse douce, moment historique de la plus grande jouissance.*

> pp. 40–1

The old values are no longer transmitted, no longer circulate, no longer impress; literature is desacralized, institutions are impotent to defend

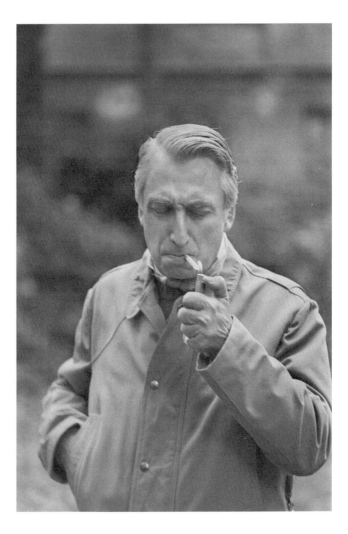

17. Left-handed.

and impose it as the implicit model of the human. It is not, if you will, that literature is destroyed; rather *it is no longer protected*: so this is the moment to go there. Literary semiology is, as it were, that journey that lands us in a country free by default; angels and dragons are no longer there to defend it. Our gaze can fall, not without perversity, upon certain old and lovely things, whose signified is abstract, out of date. It is a moment at once decadent and prophetic, a moment of gentle apocalypse, a historical moment of the greatest possible pleasure.

pp. 475–6

No single enterprise, but only Barthes's succession of disparate projects, could provide the intelligibility of this strangest moment, when what has been denigrated returns; only these disparate writings could create such possibilities of pleasure, of understanding, and renewal.

Chapter 11
Barthes after Barthes

What has happened to Barthes since his death? There have been at least three events of note. In 1987 François Wahl, who had taken on the role of Barthes's literary executor, brought out under Barthes's name a slim volume entitled *Incidents*. It consists of two very short texts and two somewhat longer ones, which share, Wahl claims, writing's effort to grasp the immediate ('se saisir de l'immédiat') (p. 7).[25] Wahl's decision to create this book provoked a good deal of controversy because the two longer texts, 'Incidents' and 'Soirées de Paris', articulate what Barthes even in his most autobiographical writings had preferred not to announce: his homosexuality. 'Incidents' itself offers snapshots of encounters in Morocco in 1968 and 1969 – most of them only a couple of sentences – in which Moroccan boys figure prominently. Loosely influenced by André Gide's journal, which had narrated homosexual encounters in North Africa, Barthes's text avoids narrative and presupposes rather than describes homosexual encounters in laconic fragments: 'Mustafa is in love with his cap. "My cap – I love it." He won't take it off to make love' (*Incidents*, p. 30/19). *Barthes par Barthes* had described the project of a book entitled '*Incidents* (mini-texts, one-liners, haiku, notations, puns, everything that falls, like a leaf)', to which this text is certainly related (p. 153/150). But precisely because 'Incidents' is so lacking in events, puns, jokes, or notations with a formal resemblance to haiku, attention is drawn to the sexual situations that might lie behind its laconic observations.

Greater interest, and greater dismay, was provoked by the journal sequence Wahl published entitled 'Soirées de Paris' but which Barthes refers to as 'Vaines soirées' (Pointless Evenings). These pages from the summer before Barthes's death recount evenings in Paris in which nothing much happens: he dines with friends, looks for a film to go to, hangs out in cafés, indecisively pursues young men, or else finds their approaches annoying, wishing he might be left alone to read his newspaper in peace. Barthes had previously reflected on the journal form in an essay entitled 'Deliberation': should I keep a journal with a view to publishing it? He runs through the disadvantages: the journal has no 'mission', no necessity; it forces the writer to strike poses, and in its triviality, inessentiality, and factitiousness incessantly opens the comic question, 'Am I?' (*Le Bruissement de la langue*, pp. 435–8/369–72). But these very disadvantages seem to attract Barthes to the journal. The notation of non-events becomes an 'almost impossible' form of writing, attractive in all the things it refuses: meaning, continuity, plot, architectonics.

In practice, though, 'Soirées de Paris' tantalizes by the half-concealment (behind initials) of friends, who were subsequently annoyed to find that evenings Barthes had spent with them qualified as 'empty'. Above all it seduces by its admission of aimlessness. The pathetic spectacle of the famous intellectual bored with his Parisian evenings and half-heartedly seeking sexual partners ends on a sombre note:

> A sort of despair overcame me, I felt like crying. How clearly I saw that I would have to give up boys, because none of them felt any desire for me, and I was either too scrupulous or too clumsy to impose my desire on them; that this is an unavoidable fact, averred by all my efforts at flirting, that I have a melancholy life, that, finally, I am bored to death by it, and that I must divest my life of this interest, or this hope. . . . Nothing will be left for me but hustlers. (But then what would I do when I go out? I keep noticing young men, immediately wanting to be in love with them. What will the spectacle of my world come to be?) – I played the piano a little

for O [a young friend Olivier he had brought home], after he asked me to, knowing at that very moment that I had given him up; how lovely his eyes were then, and his gentle face, made gentler by his long hair: a delicate but inaccessible and enigmatic creature, sweet-natured yet remote. Then I sent him away, saying I had work to do, knowing it was over, and that more than Olivier was over: the love of *one* boy.

pp. 115–16/73

This is how the book concludes: not 'no more boys' but no more possibility of love *for* or the love *of* any single boy.

If François Wahl was thought to have made a dubious decision in publishing these texts, which altered the image of Barthes, he was less forthcoming in other respects: he did not give Louis-Jean Calvet, author of a well-researched and informative biography, permission to quote from Barthes's extensive correspondence, and he refused to allow Barthes's lectures at the Collège de France to be published, even though they were completely written out and had been widely attended. When Laurent Dispot published extracts from the courses in the journal *La Règle du jeu* in 1991, the journal was sued by the heirs determined to protect the rights of this author who had declared the death of the author – an act that provoked an outpouring of support for the indicted journal from Parisian intellectuals, including Philippe Sollers and Julia Kristeva.[26]

It is frustrating, especially for those who had not been able to attend the lectures, to know that these texts on subjects Barthes had not treated in his publications are being withheld. One series, 'How to live together: novelistic simulations of some spaces of daily life' (1977), bore on novelistic representations of spaces of daily living and conventions for the organization of life, from Robinson Crusoe's hut to the hotel of *The Magic Mountain* and Zola's bourgeois apartment building. Another series treated 'le Neutre' (1978) – the neuter or neutral, the neutralizing, transcendence, or evasion of binary oppositions – which had been the

18. At the École pratique des hautes études 1973.

subject of brief ruminations in *Barthes par Barthes*. The third and fourth series both focused on 'Preparation for the novel': 'from life to work' (1978–9) and 'the work as volition' (1979–80), approaching literary creation not from the perspective of the reader but from that of the writer.[27] The first year of this course concentrated on the haiku as a form of notation of minor affect; the second, on the wish to write and the rituals it can induce, included reflections on Proust's cork-lined room, Balzac's dressing gown and inordinate consumption of coffee – particularly piquant coming from the pen of one who had previously announced that the death of the author was the price to be paid for the birth of the reader, as the agency through which one could best understand the operation of literature. One may hope that Wahl will eventually release these texts, in an attempt to stimulate continuing interest in Barthes, as has happened with the gradual, still incomplete publication of Lacan's seminars.

What has Barthes become, 20 years after his death? The simplest answer is that he has become a writer. His *Œuvres complètes* – three massive volumes of over a thousand pages each – were brought out by his longtime publisher, Éditions du Seuil (this is the third editorial event I mentioned). The main effect of this edition is to submerge the individual books by which Barthes had made his reputation in a sea of other writings: essays, prefaces, responses to interviewers' questions, lectures and précis of lectures, and many short journalistic pieces. The three volumes display a continuing production and focus attention on the thinker, the man of letters, but above all the writer who is their common source. These volumes also suggest how much Barthes liked the stimulus of a particular assignment. Though he was bad at saying 'no' and apparently always complained about the many obligations he had taken on, requests and assignments provoked him to say something interesting about a given topic and led to a production that is stylish, elegant, and resistant to received opinion – the *Doxa*.

The *Œuvres complètes* reinforced the image of Barthes as a writer by bringing together pieces that had been scattered in all sorts of publications, in France and abroad: *Le Monde*, *L'Almanacco Bompiani*, *Ça*, *Photo*, *Art Press*, *Playboy*, *Zoom*, *Nuova revista musicale italiana*, *Vogue-Homme*, not to mention numerous museum and exposition catalogues. They display very broad cultural interests, in the visual arts, music, and contemporary literature. And yet Barthes never wrote negative reviews; he does not play cultural arbiter. In fact, he is the most unpolemical of men, though he allows himself remarks that generate polemics in others. (Being forced into polemics by Picard's attack on *Sur Racine* had been a great source of unhappiness to him.) Because these writings cannot be encompassed in even the most broadly defined project, even that of cultural arbiter, they become the work of a writer.

If one had to give a name to the project, one might say that it is an anthropology of contemporary life. Barthes was interested in all sorts of practices and cultural creations, as had earlier emerged in his articles for

Mythologies in the 1950s, only subsequently his articles were not accompanied as those were by an essay outlining a theoretical programme. One of his interviews for *Playboy*, published the month of his death, discusses dieting as a religious phenomenon, with its conversions, bibles, lapses into sin, and returns to the prescribed path. 'The regimen mobilizes a keen sense of guilt, the threat of sin, which is there at every moment of the day. Only when you are sleeping are you sure of not sinning.' A book should be written, he says, 'about the phenomenon and the mythology of dieting'.[28] There is still a critical edge, but the target is more likely to be assumptions and habits of Americans (as in the dieting interview) or possibly of French intellectuals than of the French bourgeoisie, as had been the case in the days of *Mythologies*. Barthes writes that for a long time he believed that intellectuals should fight to demystify culture, and while he still fights from time to time, his heart isn't in it ('au fond je n'y crois guère'). Power is everywhere and it's the fate of the contemporary subject to be

(*) Dessin d'Orlie.

19. *Le Monde*, 14 February 1975.

recuperated. 'The only resort would be to make heard a voice that is off to one side, elsewhere, without relation.'[29] But to be without relation is a utopian wish.

For three and a half months, in 1978-9, Barthes wrote a brief weekly chronicle in the *Nouvel Observateur*, on something that had struck him – from the availability of cherries in the winter or the phenomenon of excessive packaging to a demonstration of solidarity with an imprisoned writer. He explains, as he is breaking off the experiment, that these are not another version of *Mythologies* but an experiment in writing, the quest for a form, for the recording of incidents that strike him but do not rise to the status of events. They are attempts to 'give voice to the very diverse voices that compose me'.[30] One detects the same preoccupation as in *Incidents* and in 'Preparation for the Novel': the interest in minor articulations of daily life which do not form a plot but which provide the texture of meaning. 'In the country I like to piss outside in the garden', he records. 'I would like to know what this means.'

In 1978 Barthes gave a powerful and eloquent lecture in both Paris and New York entitled 'Longtemps, je me suis couché de bonne heure'. This title is the opening line of Proust's *Remembrance of Things Past*, 'Time was, I went to bed early'. That repeating of Proust's sentence illustrates Barthes's decision to identify with Proust – not 'with the prestigious author of a monumental work but with the worker: now tormented, now exalted, in any case modest – who wanted to undertake a task upon which, from the very start of his project, he conferred an absolute character' (*Le Bruissement de la langue*, p. 334/277-8). Well into his thirties, Proust was hesitating between the novel and the essay but suddenly – we don't know why – in the summer of 1909, everything fell into place; he hit upon a 'third form' that would 'abolish the contradiction between Novel and Essay' through its handling of time and its invention of the narrator who recounts his desire to write (p. 336-40/280-4). Barthes conjectures that the event which precipitated for Proust the need for a new practice of writing was the death of his mother, and Barthes, who has just lost his own mother, presents himself as similarly situated, ready for a 'vita nova' ('You knew you were mortal; suddenly you feel mortal.'). Seeing himself condemned to repetition until death (another article, another lecture course), he writes, 'I must emerge from that shadowy state (medieval theory called it *acedia*) to which the attrition of repeated tasks and mourning dispose me. Now, for the subject who writes, who has chosen to write, there can be no "new life", it seems to me, except in the discovery of a new practice of writing' (p. 342/286).

Proust was seeking, and found, 'a form which will accommodate suffering and transcend it' (p. 335/279). Barthes finds in the episode of the death of the narrator's grandmother in Proust's *Recherche* and that of the death of Prince Bolkonsky in Tolstoy's *War and Peace* two 'moments of truth' where 'suddenly literature coincides absolutely with an emotional landslide, a "cry" in the body of the reader who suffers, in memory or anticipation, radical separation from the beloved person, a transcendence is posited: what Lucifer created *at the same time* love and death?' (p. 343/287). Though pathos is scorned today, the novel 'is precisely the form which, by delegating the discourse of affect to characters, permits saying that affect openly: here the pathetic can be said' (p. 345/289). The writer is the repository of all the world's losses, and the sentiment which should animate the work is love, or pity or compassion. This is the vision of literature that justifies choosing a *vita nova* that makes literature its all-encompassing horizon.

Does this mean, Barthes concludes, that I am going to write a novel? 'How should I know?' I do know, he says, that 'it is important for me to act *as if* I ought to write this utopian novel'. And this involves henceforth putting himself in the position 'of the subject who makes something and no longer of the subject who speaks about something. I am not studying a product, I assume a production . . . I postulate a novel to be written, whereby I can expect to learn more about the novel than

by merely considering it as an object already written by others'
(p. 345-6/289-90).

This is one of Barthes's most eloquent, moving, and insightful essays, and it has predictably provoked enthusiasm both for the novel he might have produced and for the 'preparation of the novel', as he put it in his courses. Yet its power is connected with its shrewd analysis of the novels of others, particularly Proust's technical strategies, and with its theory of the novel: for a 'pathetic' theory or history of the novel, he writes – one focusing on the articulation of pathos – we must 'no longer place a book's essence in its structure, but on the contrary acknowledge that the work moves, lives, germinates, through a kind of "collapse" which leaves only certain moments standing, moments which are strictly speaking its summits . . .' (p. 344/287). This is an important though certainly debatable claim about the novel, which prompts one to ask whether the power of these 'summits' does not in various ways depend upon their relations to other parts of the structure. At any rate, this is unmistakably a significant critical claim about the nature of finished masterpieces, not the vision of someone struggling to write. As soon as Barthes sets up an opposition – such as 'assuming a production' rather than 'studying a product' – his practice undermines it.

This compelling essay, with its announcement of a conversion to a new life, a new practice of writing, and a new perspective on writing, gives special poignancy to eight one-page outlines entitled 'Vita Nova' that were found among Barthes's papers and that are published in facsimile as the final documents of the *Œuvres complètes*. Apparently, as the title indicates, this would have been a book exploring the possibility of a conversion to a new life. Beginning with his mourning for his mother (in one version she plays the guide, as Virgil does to Dante), confronting the world as both a spectacle and an object of indifference ('Pointless Evenings' would be included here), detailing his likes and dislikes, he would then recount what he calls 'the decision of April 15, 1978'. We don't know for certain whether there was such a decision (the reduction to a single day makes one suspect a fictional device for the purposes of narrative), though the Proust essay makes the idea of a conversion quite plausible. Eric Marty's note to the transcription of one plan for 'Vita Nova' explains, 'we know nothing precise about this "decision"; it is clear, however, that mythically it is a matter of converting, in a Pascalian way, to a "new life" in which "literature" would be the entire horizon of existence.'[31] Several versions of the plan speak of literature as substitute for love, and propose to proceed to an examination of possible literary modes – essay, journal, novel, fragment, the comic, nostalgia – and their failings. The climax would come with a passage from the exercise of will (necessary to produce literature) to pure idleness or ease, 'l'Oisiveté pure', or a philosophical quietude, also known as the Tao or 'le Neutre'.[32] In one of the plans Barthes refers to Heidegger's opposition between will, which seeks to change nature, and the openness to Being, the acceptance of what is. In another he proposes to take Tolstoy as master: Tolstoy had championed a Taoist and Christian quietude which neutralizes evil by absorbing it rather than struggling against it, and Barthes speculates in a late interview, 'Dare to be Lazy!', about the virtues of this unfashionable attitude, wondering whether we don't have the right to be lazy in the face of evil.[33] The work of writing is opposed to philosophic idleness, which Barthes proposes to incarnate in the figure of the Moroccan boy – an enigmatical reference explained by a fragment in 'Incidents':

> A boy sitting on a low wall, at the side of the road, which he ignores – sitting there as though for eternity, sitting there in order to be sitting, *without equivocation*:

> 'Seated peaceably, doing nothing,
> Spring comes and the grass grows of its own accord.'

p. 57/38[34]

Would the Moroccan boy be the final emblem of a peace with the world and the self achieved through the abandonment of will, a neutrality that erases the codes, the internal dialogue and equivocation that constitutes us? If so, we would seem to have a very ambitious project with a didactic narrative, a structure with an ending! But the penultimate sketch of 'Vita Nova' notes at the end, 'This means that one should abandon the childishness of a Vita nova narrative: these efforts of the frog to puff itself up as big as [the bull].'[35]

Would Barthes have written a novel, had his new life lasted longer than 23 months? Was 'Vita Nova' the great work that Barthes would have written had not death cut him off? The celebration of an idleness defined in opposition to the will that would be required to produce any sustained work certainly complicates the question, as does our knowledge that Barthes avoided structures which signify and preferred those which compile fragments in markedly arbitrary ways – alphabetical lists, for instance. His dislike of what he called 'hysteria' would have kept him away from a plot or a structure with any dramatic character that threatened to signify.

Diana Knight, in the best study of the outlines for 'Vita Nova', argues that we should take Barthes at his word when he says in the Proust lecture that it is important for him to act *as if* he ought to write this utopian novel, not actually to write it. Planning it, sketching some fragments, is one thing. Actually writing it would betray its utopian character as well as the Zen principles to which it proposes to dedicate itself.

These questions surrounding the 'Vita Nova' and Barthes's commitment to a new life are extraordinarily interesting, especially for anyone engaged with Barthes, and a case can be made that the quest for 'le Neutre' – the neutral – is the most unifying strand of Barthes's prolific career. In *Roland Barthes: vers le neutre* Bernard Comment argues that the neutral is 'the attempt to escape the obligations and constraints of the logos, of Discourse'; 'denouncing or relativizing a practice should serve to found or approach the condition of the *Neutre*, understood as a radically Other regime of meaning.'[36] Though we can indeed track this underlying impulse in Barthes's work, it is one that is easy to satirize as escapism, as Philippe Lejeune, an expert on autobiography, does in a chapter of *Moi aussi* that parodies *Barthes par Barthes*. Here is one of a series of alphabetized fragments entitled 'Incoherent?' – like *Barthes par Barthes* describing himself in the third person:

> He began by satirizing the logic of *neither-nor* (*Mythologies*) finally to attain a utopian reverie on *le Neutre* (which is a kind of neither-nor squared).

> In his early books he separated language from reality to deprive it of its innocence. Now the same operation permits him to restore to language its innocence and protect it from any criticism. Under the name of *the imaginary* or *the novelistic* he lovingly incubates what he mocked under the name of mythology or ideology. Contradiction? Palinode? This is what opinion in the West too swiftly concludes. Rather, a drifting [*dérive*] beginning from an ambiguous position ... He is not a turncoat: mythology is the imaginary of the Other (a system of images one does not wholly share), and the imaginary is a happy mythology. For some time in the name of 'purging' himself, he has been proceeding, step by step, through his own foolishness [*bêtise*], exploring it, savoring it, trying to 'say' it; he makes books out of it.[37]

Lejeune also writes 'the bourgeois who has succeeded no longer believes in the class struggle; he loves the *le Neutre*.'[38]

Mockery of *le Neutre* as conclusion reminds us that it must not be separated from the critical work that it inspires, lest one fall into the complacency Lejeune satirizes. It may be more salutary to follow Diana Knight rather than Bernard Comment (though their perspectives are similar), and take the unifying strand in Barthes as the utopian rather than the quest for *le Neutre*: theory and criticism work always through the implicit image of a social or affective utopia, in relation to which realities and discourses are found wanting.[39] The mistake would be to imagine the utopia as attainable.

The changes that the 20 years since Barthes's death have brought may be summed up under five headings.

First, there has been a massive shift in his importance. In 1979, a year before his death, Wayne Booth called Barthes 'the man who may well be the strongest influence on American criticism today'. This was meant, I should stipulate, less as praise of Barthes than as a complaint about the nefarious temptations to which American criticism was seen as succumbing, but still, it is a statement that, read in 2001, brings you up short, reminding you of the importance Barthes had in the 1970s. That importance is hard to describe, and that in itself is interesting. It certainly wasn't the importance of what Foucault calls the founder of a 'discursivity', such as Freud or Marx, where attempts to advance thought take the form of commentaries on or interpretations of the original texts. Nor was it the importance of the founder of a school, who had established a theoretical framework within which lots of people were working (there weren't in Britain or America 'Barthians' the way there are Lacanians or Althusserians, though there were many people, including me, who had been greatly influenced by Barthes). Nor was it the importance of a discoverer, who is routinely credited with an important insight, the way in which, say, Benedict Anderson is routinely cited for showing us that nations and other large communities are all 'imagined communities'. The mark of the special kind of importance Barthes had was that his authority could serve as a starting point that required no justification: 'Roland Barthes remarks that . . .' was a good way of starting an essay on almost any topic; his importance consisted precisely in the fact that no one would say 'so what?'

This is an authority that in literary studies Walter Benjamin has subsequently acquired (with the difference that Benjamin also represents a textual corpus that people devote themselves to explicating). This authority of the uncontested reference point, as one might call it, makes someone a major thinker and cultural figure, but Barthes has to a large extent lost this strange sort of authority. He is no longer someone you can just cite to get things underway. Today, one needs to say why one reads or quotes him.

Second, it was easy to see Barthes as above all a theorist in the heyday of what was called just 'theory' for short, but now that 'high theory' is no longer new, no longer so feared and admired, Barthes can easily take on importance as one who resisted theory – especially his own theories – and sought to evade or outplay it. I shall return to this issue shortly.

Third, Barthes's admirers are less likely today to celebrate restlessness or change as the constant of his work: more constants have appeared, despite the protean evolution, whether they are the utopian impulse (Knight), the quest for *le Neutre* (Comment), or the attempt to make knowledge literary (Philippe Roger). But do these constants capture what is most interesting about Barthes?

Fourth, Barthes's interest in writing the body can now be seen as belonging, D. A. Miller writes, to the 'gay male cultural project of resurrecting the flesh, to which it adds (or in which it brings out) certain valuable nuances', especially the willingness to 'conceive of this body in its most embarrassed state, devoid of anything that might be called "finish"'.[40] The process of claiming Barthes for a gay aesthetic is barely underway.

Finally, and most important perhaps, this once radical figure, the threat to the values of French culture, has become an icon for many of the values he once seemed most to threaten. In June 2000, an article in *Télérama* (a cross between *TV Guide* and the *New York Times Book Review*) entitled 'The Emperor of Signs' recalled him with this heading:

'Lover of language, idolater of the sentence, this writer used sociology and psychoanalysis but above all an uncommon subtlety, to illuminate French literature,'[41] No trace here of the champion of the avant-garde, critic of bourgeois myths, bête noir of the Sorbonne, scandalmonger who proclaimed the death of the author. Also elided here is semiology, replaced by sociology; and this is not just a mistake, as one sees later when semiology is mentioned as something he abandoned. Barthes is 'un amoureux fou de notre langue, un possedé de ses finesses' (head-over-heels in love with our language, obsessed by its finer points), which is quite a respectable thing to be in France, only a bit comical, certainly not outrageous or dangerous.

Barthes has become a cultural icon whose passage through other supposedly radical phases to the love of the French language and its subtleties makes him all the more valuable as a confirmation that culture resides essentially in the relation of the individual subject to a patrimony best represented by the mother tongue. 'Having abandoned the scientific illusions of hard-line structuralism, rid of the slogans of political and cultural militancies, our semiologist began a new life of writing. Barthes henceforth lets Roland speak, bringing to the forefront the desiring subject, his singular self, unabashed lover of language and style.'

I cite this not because it is contemptible, but because it is at once typical and easily justified by the trajectory of Barthes's writings. As we have seen, the late writings chide his 'euphoric dream of scientificity'. The metalanguage of binary oppositions that had played crucial roles in earlier analyses even as they were being put into question – *denotation* versus *connotation*, *metaphor* versus *metonymy*, *readerly* versus *writerly* – are mocked in *Barthes par Barthes* as 'forgeries', 'figures of production', or 'textual operators' stolen from other discourses and used as part of the 'machine of writing', to 'make the text go' (p. 95/92). 'Hence the work proceeds by conceptual infatuations, successive enthusiasms, perishable manias' (p. 114/110).

20. Jacket photo from Louis-Jean Calvet's biography *Roland Barthes*.

It is tempting to adopt this posture of knowingness, and celebrate the superior insight of the writer rather than the delusions of the would-be theorist. This posture is very seductive, especially today, when the prestige of theory has worn off and to be a savvy critic of the pretensions of theory seems a more winning posture. But precisely because of the seductiveness of this view, the thinking reader needs to reflect on its implications – a reflection that might take two possible directions. First, one might ask, as I have done earlier, whether Barthes's apparent demystification of his past work is not a remystification, a stylish evasion. Given the difficulty of assessing one's past concepts, how tempting to declare them infatuations or manifestations of an underlying desire to write that might link one with other authors. No theory here, just writing! Barthes's mocking of his past concepts may work to create, precisely, a Barthian myth, the myth of the writer, the author.

This is not to say that Barthes wasn't a writer: he is an extraordinarily distinctive one: elegant, idiosyncratic, boldly undefensive. But just as he argued that wine is objectively good but the goodness of wine is a myth, one should aver that while Barthes is objectively a great writer, Barthes the writer is a myth – an ideological construction whose effect is precisely to discourage one from picking up and testing his formulations, using them to see what they do with the cultural objects and practices we are interested in analysing. Barthes wanted to write, he declared, not *write about*, but the greatness and interest of his writing is inseparable from the claims it makes about the cultural objects he addresses, and this is just as true in the superb late essay on Proust, where he declares his conversion from writing on subjects to just *writing*, as it is in earlier works (which also frequently embraced the idea of production).

The denigration of past concepts or theorizations and the celebration of Barthes as writer are thus two sides of the same coin, and it is important to reflect on their consequences for the value of Barthes today. Why should one read him? To heighten one's suspicion that theoretical discourse is really just a dubious form of self-aggrandizement? Then the value of Barthes would depend upon there being a powerful presence of theory which one needed to learn to resist, which is scarcely the case. On the contrary, Barthes's work serves better to alert us to the adventures of thought and to encourage the attempt to think outside of received opinion.

I would contend that the value, nay, the genius of Barthes lies not in the blend of knowingness or sentimentality of the late work but in the early work, which tries out possible sciences. In *Essais critiques* he calls the writer a public experimenter, who tries out ideas in public, for the public (p. 10/xii). In *Barthes par Barthes* he reverts to this idea: he [Barthes] 'invokes notions; modernity is tried (the way one tries all the buttons on a radio one doesn't know how to work' (p. 78/74).

An essential feature of Barthes's genius is to have discovered the heuristic function of systematicity and of the requirement of explicitness. It is precisely when he was trying to produce a systematic theory or analysis of something that he was led, by this procedure, to take on problems, topics, elements in discourse that are usually passed over. The semiotic model, in positing that where there is meaning there is system and that one must identify the different levels of signification and the signifiers and signifieds for every level of signification, required him to think, for instance, about the function of every element in fashion captions and about how, say, social class is reflected in remarks about the weather. In the case of literature, the step-by-step procedure of *S/Z* forced him to reflect explicitly on how details, both the most apparently insignificant as well as the most telling, are picked up, assimilated, organized, according to what models or codes.

Systematicity is, first and foremost, a means of estrangement, *Verfremdung*. You have to look at things in new pieces, new ways, and come up with something to say. So whether or not a genuine theory takes shape, the systematizing drive is crucial for Barthes, and when he turns against it, he risks lapsing into the bourgeois and sentimental forms of mythifying whose mechanisms he had analysed.

An instance of the virtues of systematicity is the very simple and accessible line of reflection (now a staple in the French educational system) on what Barthes called 'l'effet de réel' (the reality effect). He starts from a barometer hanging on the wall in the Aubains' house in Flaubert's 'Un cœur simple': 'Underneath a barometer, an old piano bore a pyramid-shaped pile of boxes and cartons.' What of the barometer? Barthes asks. 'If analysis seeks to be exhaustive', he writes, '(and what would any method be worth which did not account for the totality of its object, i.e. in this case of the entire surface of the narrative fabric?) . . . it inevitably encounters notations which no function (not even the most indirect) can justify . . .' (*Le Bruissement de la langue*, pp. 179–80/141). They involve a kind of banal excess, a 'luxe' of narration. There arises here, Barthes writes, a question which has the greatest importance for the structural analysis of narrative: 'Is everything in narrative significant and, if not, if insignificant stretches subsist in the narrative syntagm, what is ultimately, so to speak, the significance of this insignificance?' (p. 181/143). Details that do not contribute to plot, suspense, character, atmosphere, or symbolic meaning, nevertheless have a signifying function, he concludes: by their very absence of meaning they signify, 'we are the real', since in Western ideology there is an opposition between meaning and reality, 'a great mythic opposition of the true-to-life and the intelligible'. 'The irreducible residues of functional analysis have this in common; they denote what is ordinarily called "concrete reality"' (p. 184/146). This very important function in semiotic systems had not been theorized, not conceived as a connotative function, yet it is crucial both to works of the realist tradition and the avant-garde, as Barthes theorized it in Robbe-Grillet in particular, where description purges meaning (through an excess of detail and objectivity) and breaks the fascination of narrative.

It is the semiological commitment that enables Barthes to identify the constant struggle between meaning and its evacuation in literature, fashion, and other signifying systems, where it is all too easy for a humanistic criticism to presume the presence of sufficient meaning without worrying about the millions of signs that gesture toward meaning while failing to deliver what is expected.

The task of literature, Barthes writes in the preface to *Essais critiques*, is not as is often thought 'to express the unexpressible' – this would be a literature of the soul – but 'to unexpress the expressible' (*inexprimer l'exprimable*), to problematize the meanings our cultural codes otherwise confer, and thus to unwrite the world as it is written by prior discursive practices (p. 15/xvii). Thus there is a link between the goals of the champion of the avant-garde, of cultural transformation, and that euphoric dream of scientificity that led the younger Barthes to attempt a systematic semiology and to attend in particular to whatever we take for granted or treat as unimportant. It would be a pity if this Barthes were forever lost in the image of the 'unabashed lover of language and of style' promoted by Barthes's modern admirers, who want to forget the theorist for the writer. The theorist, one should say rather, is the writer whose ideas one takes seriously. This much Barthes surely deserves.

Notes and references

1 Wayne Booth, *Critical Understanding* (University of Chicago Press, 1979), p. 69.

2 John Sturrock, 'Roland Barthes', in *Structuralism and Since* (Oxford University Press, 1979), p. 52.

3 Jean-Paul Sartre, *Qu'est-ce que la littérature?* (Gallimard, 1948), pp. 334, 345, 341; *What is Literature?* (Methuen, 1970), pp. 206, 212–13, 210.

4 In *Essais critiques* Barthes replaces Sartre's distinction between poet and prose writer by a distinction between *écrivain* and *écrivant*. The *écrivain* is engaged in an exploration of language, while the *écrivant* uses it to write up or write out his message. For Barthes, all interesting writers are *écrivains*.

5 In a 1971 interview ('Réponses', pp. 92–3) Barthes says he was attempting in *Le Degré zéro* to 'Marxianize the Sartrean commitment'. Unfortunately, one cannot wholly trust his recollections here, since he also claims that in 1953 he had never heard of Maurice Blanchot, who in fact appears prominently in *Le Degré zéro*: a statement of his on Kafka is quoted and his work on Mallarmé is cited as the source of Barthes's own views.

6 Barthes, 'Maîtres et esclaves', *Lettres nouvelles* (March 1953), p. 108.

7 Barthes speaks of his love for 'scription', the act of writing: 'Writing is the hand and thus the body: its impulses, controlling mechanisms, rhythms, weighings, slidings, complications,

evasions – in short, not the *soul* but the subject ballasted by its desire and its unconscious' (*Le Grain de la voix*, p. 184/193). He also says that in writers of earlier periods there is 'a chance of avant-garde' 'whenever it's the body that writes and not ideology' (p. 182/191). For further discussion, see Chapter 8.

8 See *Le Plaisir du texte*, which explains that the reader accedes to *jouissance* (the pleasure offered by the radical text) through the *cohabitation* of languages working side by side (p. 10/4). Barthes notes that he had already discovered this cohabitation in Sade: 'antipathetic codes (the noble and the trivial, for example) come into contact, pompous and ridiculous neologisms are created; pornographic messages are embodied in sentences so pure that they might be used as grammatical models' (p. 14/6). Barthes's reading, adding its own language, accentuates these effects of collision.

9 Raymond Picard, *Nouvelle critique ou nouvelle imposture?* (Pauvert, 1965), p. 69; *New Criticism or New Fraud?*, tr. Frank Towne (Washington State University Press, 1969), p. 21.

10 Édouard Guitton, 'M. Barthes et la critique universitaire', *Le Monde*, 28 March 1964, p. 9.

11 For discussion of Saussure's theory of language and his proposals for semiology, see my *Saussure* (Fontana, 1976); revised edition: *Ferdinand de Saussure* (Cornell University Press, 1986).

12 See my *Structuralist Poetics: Structuralism, Linguistics, and the Study of Literature* (Cornell University Press, 1975), pp. 34–8.

13 For general discussion of the use of linguistics in structuralist literary studies, see my *Structuralist Poetics*, part 1. For Barthes's use of Benveniste's distinction, see pp. 197–200.

14 Barthes, 'Par où commencer?', in *Le Degré zéro, suivi de Nouveaux essais critiques*, p. 155/*New Critical Essays*, p. 89. This essay is Barthes's nearest approximation to instructions for undertaking a structural analysis.

15 See Barthes's 'Analyse textuelle d'un conte d'Edgar Poe', in *L'Aventure sémiologique*.

16   In a brilliant discussion contrasting Barthes's 'anti-constructionist' approach to *Sarrasine* with a 'deconstructionist' reading, Barbara Johnson argues that his refusal to reorder or reconstruct the text leads him to miss ways in which the work undermines the presuppositions of the readerly mode to which it supposedly belongs. See her essay 'The Critical Difference: BartheS/BalZac', in *The Critical Difference* (Johns Hopkins Press, 1981).

17   See Barthes's 'L'Effet de réel,' *Le Bruissement de la langue*, pp. 185-6/146-7.

18   For an explanation of deconstruction, see my *On Deconstruction: Theory and Criticism after Structuralism* (Cornell University Press, 1982).

19   Preface to Chateaubriand's *Vie de Rancé*, in *Le Degré zéro de l'écriture, suivi de Nouveaux essais critiques*, p. 106/*New Critical Essays*, p. 41.

20   Michel-Antoine Burnier and Patrick Rambaud, *Le Roland-Barthes sans peine* (Ballard, 1978), p. 41.

21   'To Write: an Intransitive Verb', *Le Bruissement de la langue*, pp. 21-31/11-21.

22   For a semiotic discussion of the sentimental, see my *Flaubert: The Uses of Uncertainty* (Cornell University Press, 1974), pp. 225-8.

23   Particularly interesting are 'The Wisdom of Art', introduction to *Cy Twombly, Paintings and Drawings, 1954-1977*, catalogue of an exhibition at the Whitney Museum of American Art (New York, 1979), collected in *The Responsibility of Forms*, pp. 157-76, and 'Lecture de Brillat-Savarin', preface to a re-edition of Brillat-Savarin's *La Physiologie du goût* (Hermann, 1975), in *The Rustle of Language*, pp. 250-70.

24   For discussion of this problem, see my *On Deconstruction* (Cornell University Press, 1982), chapter 1.

25   François Wahl's preface does not appear in the English translation.

26   See *La Règle du jeu* 5 (1991). Statements of support are published in 6 (1992). See also *L'Infini* 37 (1992).

27   For brief summaries of three of these lecture series, see *Œuvres*

complètes, vol. 3 (Seuil, 1995): 'Comment vivre ensemble', p. 744, 'Le Neutre', p. 887, 'La Préparation du roman (1): de la vie à l'œuvre', p. 1059. The topic of 'le neutre', as a goal which gives coherence to the diversity of Barthes's writing, is ably explored in Bernard Comment, *Roland Barthes: vers le neutre* (Christian Bourgois, 1991).

28 'Entretien', *Œuvres complètes*, vol. 3, p. 1241. For such a book, see Richard Klein, *Eat Fat* (Pantheon, 1996).

29 'Démystifier', La Chronique, *Œuvres complètes*, vol. 3, p. 988.

30 'Pause', La Chronique, *Œuvres complètes*, vol. 3, pp. 990–1.

31 'Vita Nova', *Œuvres complètes*, vol. 3, p. 1300, note 2.

32 Ibid., p. 1301.

33 Ibid., p. 1302. See also 'Osons être paresseux!' *Œuvres complètes*, vol. 3, p. 1085.

34 Diana Knight, in the best discussion of 'Vita Nova', explains the Moroccan boy by identifying this passage in 'Incidents' and the Zen poem here quoted, from the *Zenrin Kushu*, which Barthes takes from Alan Watts's *The Way of Zen*. Eric Marty in the *Œuvres complètes* wrongly transcribes Barthes's reference to 'Moroccan boy of the Zenzin poem', and then explains in a note that this must refer to a poem from Moroccan oral tradition. In fact, the Zen poem is also cited from Watts at the end of *A Lover's Discourse*. See Diana Knight, 'Idle Thoughts: Barthes's *Vita Nova*', *Nottingham French Studies* (spring 1997), pp. 94–5.

35 'Vita Nova', *Œuvres complètes*, vol. 3, p. 1306. The allusion is to La Fontaine's fable of 'The Frog who Wanted to Make Himself as Big as the Bull' (I, 3).

36 Bernard Comment, *Roland Barthes: vers le neutre* (Christian Bourgois, 1991), pp. 14, 27.

37 Philippe Lejeune, *Moi aussi* (Seuil, 1986), p. 107. The parodic chapter 'Le Roland-Barthes sans peine' is pp. 103–16.

38 Ibid., p. 108.

39 Diana Knight, *Barthes and Utopia: Space, Travel, Writing* (Oxford University Press, 1997).

40 D. A. Miller, *Bringing out Roland Barthes* (University of California Press, 1992), pp. 31–2.

41 Gilles Macassar, 'L'Empereur des signes', *Télérama* 2631 (14 June 2000), p. 62.

Notes and references

Further reading

Works by Roland Barthes

Here I list only books and one important interview. For bibliographies of Barthes's numerous articles, now collected in his *Œuvres complètes*, see *Communications* 36 (1982); Sanford Freedman and Carol Anne Taylor, *Roland Barthes: A Bibliographical Reader's Guide* (Garland, 1983); and Gilles Philippe, *Roland Barthes, Bibliographie des écrivains de France* (Memini, 1996). Philippe's excellent bibliography, while hard to find, is particularly thorough in describing writings about Barthes.

Barthes's *Œuvres complètes*, in three volumes, edited by Eric Marty, were published by Seuil in 1993, 1994, and 1995. All of the works listed below can be found in them, but my page references in this book are to the earlier individual volumes: the first to the French original, the second to the English translation. (I give page references to the English translations published in the United States, mostly by Hill and Wang, but many of these have also been issued in England by Jonathan Cape.) Entries marked with an asterisk are collections published after Barthes's death.

* *A Barthes Reader*, ed. Susan Sontag (Hill and Wang, 1982)
* *L'Aventure sémiologique* (Seuil, 1985). *The Semiotic Challenge*, tr. Richard Howard (Hill and Wang, 1988)

* *Le Bruissement de la langue* (Seuil, 1984). *The Rustle of Language*, tr. Richard Howard (Hill and Wang, 1986)

La Chambre claire: note sur la photographie (Gallimard and Seuil, 1980). *Camera Lucida: Reflections on Photography*, tr. Richard Howard (Hill and Wang, 1981)

Critique et vérité (Seuil, 1966). *Criticism and Truth*, tr. Katrine Kueneman (University of Minnesota Press, 1987)

Le Degré zéro de l'écriture (1953), with *Nouveaux essais critiques* (Seuil, 1972). *Writing Degree Zero*, tr. Annette Lavers and Colin Smith (Hill and Wang, 1968); *New Critical Essays*, tr. Richard Howard (Hill and Wang, 1980)

Éléments de sémiologie (1964), in *Le Degré zéro de l'écriture, suivi de Éléments de sémiologie* (Seuil, 1965). *Elements of Semiology*, tr. Annette Lavers and Colin Smith (Hill and Wang, 1968)

L'Empire des signes (Skira, 1970). *Empire of Signs*, tr. Richard Howard (Hill and Wang, 1982)

Essais critiques (Seuil, 1964). *Critical Essays*, tr. Richard Howard (Northwestern University Press, 1972)

Fragments d'un discours amoureux (Seuil, 1977). *A Lover's Discourse: Fragments*, tr. Richard Howard (Hill and Wang, 1978)

* *Le Grain de la voix: Entretiens 1962–1980* (Seuil, 1981). *The Grain of the Voice: Interviews 1962–1980*, tr. Linda Coverdale (Hill and Wang, 1985)

Image, Music, Text, essays selected and tr. Stephen Heath (Hill and Wang, 1977)

* *Incidents* (Seuil, 1987). *Incidents*, tr. Richard Howard (University of California Press, 1992)

Leçon: Leçon inaugurale de la chaire de sémiologie littéraire du Collège de France, prononcée le 7 janvier 1977 (Seuil, 1978). 'Inaugural Lecture', tr. Richard Howard, in *A Barthes Reader*, ed. Susan Sontag (Hill and Wang, 1982)

Michelet par lui-même (Seuil, 1954). *Michelet*, tr. Richard Howard (Blackwell, 1987)

Mythologies (1957) (Seuil, 1970). Partial translation: *Mythologies*, tr.

Annette Lavers (Hill and Wang, 1973). Translation of remaining essays: *The Eiffel Tower and Other Mythologies*, tr. Richard Howard (Hill and Wang, 1979)

Nouveaux essais critiques, published with *Le Degré zéro de l'écriture* (Paris, Seuil, 1972). *New Critical Essays*, tr. Richard Howard (Hill and Wang, 1980)

* *L'Obvie et l'obtus* (Seuil, 1982). *The Responsibility of Forms*, tr. Richard Howard (Hill and Wang, 1986)

Le Plaisir du texte (Seuil, 1973). *The Pleasure of the Text*, tr. Richard Miller (Hill and Wang, 1975)

'Réponses' (interview), *Tel Quel* 47 (autumn 1971), pp. 89–107

Roland Barthes par Roland Barthes (Seuil, 1975). *Roland Barthes by Roland Barthes*, tr. Richard Howard (Hill and Wang, 1977)

S/Z (Seuil, 1970). *S/Z*, tr. Richard Miller (Hill and Wang, 1975)

Sade/Fourier/Loyola (Seuil, 1971). *Sade/Fourier/Loyola*, tr. Richard Miller (New York, Hill and Wang, 1976)

Sollers écrivain (Seuil, 1979). *Sollers Writer*, tr. Philip Thody (Athlone Press, 1987)

Sur Racine (Seuil, 1963). *On Racine*, tr. Richard Howard (Hill and Wang, 1964)

Système de la mode (Seuil, 1967). *The Fashion System*, tr. Matthew Ward and Richard Howard (Hill and Wang, 1983)

Works on Barthes

There are now many books on Barthes. Those mentioned below are just a selection. Louis-Jean Calvet's *Roland Barthes* (Flammarion, 1990), translated by Sarah Wykes, *Roland Barthes, A Biography* (Indiana University Press, 1995), is a lively biography with lots of information about Barthes's friendships and opinions but which treats theories as feeble attempts to rationalize feelings.

Books in English

Annette Lavers' early *Roland Barthes: Structuralism and After* (Harvard University Press, 1982) can be supplemented by Michael Moriarty's

Roland Barthes (Polity Press, 1991), a clear overview, especially helpful on Barthes's dealings with Brecht and with narrative, and Stephen Ungar's *Roland Barthes: The Professor of Desire* (University of Nebraska Press, 1983), which shrewdly charts Barthes's shifting commitments and his appeal. More specialized are Andrew Brown's *Roland Barthes: The Figures of Writing* (Oxford University Press, 1992), a study of major concerns and operations in Barthes's writing; Armine Kotin Mortimer, *The Gentlest Law: Roland Barthes's 'The Pleasure of the Text'*, an exemplary, multi-dimensional reading of this book; and Diana Knight's *Barthes and Utopia: Space, Travel, Writing* (Oxford University Press, 1997), a subtle exploration of the forms of the important utopian impulse in Barthes's writing. D. A. Miller's *Bringing out Barthes* (University of California Press, 1992) obliquely but boldly evokes the gay Barthes that might have been.

Books in French

Stephen Heath's early *Vertige du déplacement: Lecture de Barthes* (Fayard, 1974) is still smart and pertinent. Philippe Roger's *Roland Barthes: roman* (Grasset, 1986) is a life and works particularly strong on Barthes's formative experiences. It is devoted to the proposition that from the outset Barthes sought to make knowledge literary. Vincent Jouve's *La Littérature selon Barthes* (Minuit, 1986) is an attempt at theoretical synthesis of Barthes's account of literature. Bernard Comment's excellent *Roland Barthes: vers le neutre* (Christian Bourgois, 1991) finds a coherent project in the utopian attempt to escape from constraints of critical as well as orthodox thinking.

Other

Prétexte: Roland Barthes (Union générale d'éditions, 1978) is the proceedings of a conference on Barthes at Cérisy, in which Barthes took an active part. *Paragraph* 11:2 (1988), *Barthes après Barthes*, ed. Cathrine Coquio and Regis Salado (Publications de l'Université de Pau, 1993), and *The Yale Journal of Criticism* (fall 2001) collect papers from other conferences on Barthes.

Numerous journals have devoted special issues to Barthes: *Tel Quel* 47 (autumn 1971), *Critique* 302 (January 1972), *Arc* 56 (1974), *Visible Language* (autumn 1977), *Studies in Twentieth-Century Literature* (spring 1981), *Poétique* 47 (September 1981), *Communications* 63 (1996), and *Nottingham French Studies* (spring 1997).

A parody of Barthes by Michel-Antoine Burnier and Patrick Rambaud, *Le Roland-Barthes sans peine* (Ballard, 1978), has rewarding moments. For further discussion of Barthes in the context of French structuralism, see Jonathan Culler, *Structuralist Poetics: Structuralism, Linguistics and the Study of Literature* (Cornell University Press, 1975).

Index

Index

Expand your collection of
VERY SHORT INTRODUCTIONS

Visit the
VERY SHORT
INTRODUCTIONS
Web site

www.oup.co.uk/vsi

➤ **Information** about all published titles

➤ News of **forthcoming books**

➤ **Extracts** from the books, including titles
not yet published

➤ **Reviews** and views

➤ **Links** to other **web sites** and main
OUP web page

➤ Information about **VSIs in translation**

➤ **Contact** the editors

➤ **Order** other **VSIs** on-line